New England Monthly
Guide to the Restaurants
of New England

New England Monthly Guide to the Restaurants of New England

Edited by Julie Michaels

Little, Brown and Company

Boston • Toronto

FIRST EDITION

LOC #87-80541

*Published simultaneously in Canada
by Little, Brown & Company (Canada) Limited*

PRINTED IN THE UNITED STATES OF AMERICA

Acknowledgments

THIS GUIDE reflects the efforts of a troupe of fine people. In addition to our dedicated restaurant critics, who must remain nameless, I would like to thank Karen Donovan for manuscript preparation, Hans Teensma and Mike Grinley for their design talents, Walker Rumble for typesetting, Carol Cioe for copyediting, Catherine Monk, Katharine Whittemore, and Susan Zesiger for their editorial help, Nina Dudley-Adams for her mapmaking skills, and Lisa Newman for keeping us on schedule. Special thanks to Daniel Okrent, whose appetite is legendary, and to Jennifer Josephy for being a most patient editor.

—*J.M.*

Burlington

**Burlington &
Green Mountains**

**White
Mountains**

Upper Valley

N. Conway

Portland

Maine Coast

Hanover

Woodstock

Portland & Southern Maine Coast

Concord

Manchester

Portsmouth

Southern Vermont

Brattleboro

Keene

Southern New Hampshire

Berkshires

Northampton

Worcester

Pioneer Valley

Boston

Greater Boston

Springfield

Worcester

Litchfield

Hartford

Providence

Cape Cod

**Litchfield
County**

Hartford

Old Lyme

Martha's Vineyard

Newport

Nantucket

New Haven

**Fairfield
County**

**Southeastern
Connecticut**

**Providence
& Newport**

**New
Haven**

Contents

Introduction

S INCE *New England Monthly* began publication in April 1984, we have printed more than one thousand reviews of restaurants in the six New England states. Conceived as a service for readers living and traveling in the region, our brief, opinionated — and, one hopes, occasionally irreverent — reviews have become one of the most popular and best read features in the magazine. Three hundred of those reviews are included in this guide.

Our reviews are written by a group of fifteen critics who dine out several times a month for the magazine. Because reviewers live in the regions they write about — and because all of them are very hungry people — we are able to follow closely the ebb and flow of restaurant fashion, and to uncover the small, out-of-the-way places that only natives know about. You won't, however, find the names of our critics listed anywhere in this book. They remain anonymous, and all of their meals are paid for by *New England Monthly*.

The ultimate test of a restaurant is the food on your plate. Each of our reviews includes some sense of the type and quality of meal you can expect to have. But each review also tries to capture the essence of a dining experience, the unique combination of food, ambience, and service that makes for an enjoyable evening out.

Price ranges mentioned here are based on the average cost of a meal for one, including appetizer, main course, dessert, tax, and tip in the winter of 1986–1987. *Inexpensive* means under $6; *Moderate* up to $18; *Expensive* up to $30; and *Very Expensive* denotes meals that cost $30 and above. Acceptance of credit cards is indicated by: AE (American Express), CB (Carte Blanche), DC (Diners Club), MC (MasterCard),

V (VISA), Cr (all major credit cards), or N (no cards accepted).

We have checked and rechecked the days and hours of service for every restaurant included in this guide. But many, especially those in resort areas, change their schedules with the seasons. Please call in advance to be sure a restaurant is open.

Restaurant reviewing is no science; ultimately, a guide like this is a compilation of opinion. It may be educated, cultivated opinion, but it is opinion nonetheless. We hope that our tastes coincide with your own, and that this guide will direct you to many memorable meals you otherwise might have missed. If you disagree, let us know. If you have a favorite restaurant we have overlooked, tell us about it; future editions of this guide are already being planned.

Julie Michaels
New England Monthly
132 Main Street
Haydenville, Massachusetts
01039

Boston

W HAT YOU might expect in a Japanese restaurant but don't get at Agatha: discreet samisen music, sushi (at least, not much), rice-paper partitions. What you do get: delicate skewers of meat, fish, and vegetables grilled over special charcoal and served in charming black boxes; hypnotic, sexy synthesizer music; and a TV silently playing Japanese videos. It's an odd place (named for Agatha Christie, the owner's favorite author), but the unusual Kyoto-style cuisine is appetizing and fun to eat. You can order combination plates or have your meal by the skewer. And you can always watch TV if you're dining solo. **(617) 262-9790. Wine, beer, sake. Lunch Tue–Sat 12–2. Dinner Tue–Sun 5–10:30. Closed Mon. Reservations recommended. Moderate to expensive. AE, DC, MC, V.**

Agatha

142 Berkeley St, Boston

Allegro

939 Boylston St, Boston

I T'S OUR CONTENTION that Allegro has the best bar in Boston. Intelligently laid out, beautifully designed — in foamy tones of aqua — this is an adult scene where you can sip a drink, wait for friends, and groove to Charlie Parker without feeling, well, intimidated. The dining room is too big and often noisy, but we have no quarrel with the efficient service or the culinary decor. From the first bite of walnut-stuffed ravioli in a Gorgonzola sauce on through to an extraordinary rabbit in puff pastry, we feel coddled, nay, embraced by a chef who is every bit as good as his architect. **(617) 891-5486. Lunch Tue–Fri 11:30–2:30. Dinner Tue–Sun 6–10:30, Fri–Sat until 11. Sun brunch 12–3. Closed Mon. Reservations recommended. Expensive. AE, MC, V.**

Annie B

651 Boylston St, Boston

F EW PLEASURES can compare with a gossip session at Annie B's glassed-in bijou of a bay window, which looks out upon the madding crowds of Boylston Street. Let the business types who predominate attend to their networking. We come here to get silly on champagne-by-the-glass and to nibble nonchalantly at the salads: warm *chèvre* slathered with aioli or fresh seafood abundant with shrimp. The sandwiches tend to be too peasanty (if one's purpose is to pick, not stuff face), but the pastas and greenery are always impeccable. **(617)**

236-2203. Mon–Thur 11:30–11, Fri–Sat until 11:30. Sun brunch 10:30–4. Reservations recommended. Moderate to expensive. AE, DC, MC, V.

....

Another Season

97 Mt. Vernon St, Boston

WE ALWAYS feel vaguely French dining at Another Season. Perhaps it's because of the murals à la Maxim's, or the intimacy of the tiny dining rooms, or the elegance of the clientele. It may even be the food, always different enough so you know that chef-owner Odette Bery hasn't lost her flair. The Chicken Normand and saffron-sauced scallops served on a bed of leeks are particular favorites. One quibble: what used to be called "ladies' portions." (617) 367-0880. Lunch Tue–Fri 12–2. Dinner Mon–Sat 6–10. Reservations recommended. Moderate to expensive. AE, MC, V.

....

Aujourd'Hui

Four Seasons Hotel, 200 Boylston St, Boston

PERHAPS it's the view of the Public Gardens, or the elegant European-style service, or the pretty variety of the Royal Doulton china. Whatever the reason, lunching at Aujourd'Hui in the ultra-classy Four Seasons Hotel is a bit like spending an afternoon in London or Paris — one feels so above the fray. The champagne sauce studded with caviar made a pretty setting for red snapper; the fist-sized oysters are fish-market fresh. But beware the chef's well-intentioned low-cal alternatives: grapefruit dressing does absolutely nothing for a lobster and papaya salad. **(617) 338-4400. Breakfast Sun–Fri 7–11, Sat until 12:30. Lunch Mon–Fri 11:30–2:30, Sun from 11. Dinner daily 6–11. Reservations recommended. Very expensive. Cr.**

Autre Chose

1105 Massachusetts Ave, Cambridge

AUTRE CHOSE has for years been a reliable source of middle-budget *cuisine bourgeoise*. The atmosphere is *intime,* perhaps a tad less than precious, and the kitchen keeps turning out Cordon Bleu classics. A memorable adventure is the smoked duck, tucked in a kiwi-juniper sauce. Best of all, the bill won't break your bank. **(617) 661-0852. Breakfast Mon–Fri 7:30–11, Sat 9–11:30. Lunch Mon–Fri 11:30–3. Dinner Mon–Thur 5:30–10, Fri–Sat until 11. Sun brunch 9–3. Reservations recommended. Expensive. Cr.**

Back Bay Bistro

565 Boylston St, Boston

A DEFINITE STANDOUT on the Newbury-Boylston streets grazing-and-gazing circuit, the Back Bay Bistro can veer from sublime to sloppy. On the celestial side: mussels seasoned to the max, with surprise hints of anise, and an oriental chicken salad so cunningly spiced that the canned mandarin slices go almost unnoticed. But there's no excuse for poppy cake topped with strawberry puree apparently plucked from the freezer — this at a time when fresh berries were abundant. Such shortcuts can undercut even the best of pretensions. **(617) 536–4477. Lunch Mon–Fri 11:30–2:30. Dinner daily 5:30–10:30. Reservations recommended. Moderate to expensive. Cr.**

....

The Blue Diner

178 Kneeland St, Boston

AT LAST we've found a high-concept restaurant that's strictly low concept: The Blue Diner serves up dishes your mom would have made had she attended a very good white-trash cooking school. Although everything could use more spice, the Mississippi barbecue, the burgers, and the macaroni-and-cheese are toothsome and the breakfasts great. The hipoisie who reopened the place haven't overdone the nostalgia bit: there are a few fancified offerings (like salmon chowder and crabcakes), but grease is happily at a minimum and the decor is genuine diner, not some souped-up protopunk fantasy of working-class life. **(617) 338–4639. Beer and wine. Mon–Thur 6 a.m.–10 p.m., Fri until midnight, Sat 8 a.m.–midnight, Sun 10 a.m.–4. Moderate. AE, MC, V.**

....

Bnu

123 Stuart St (City Pl), Boston

BNU'S DECOR takes the cake for postmodern cutesiness (it looks like a tiny Italian village vandalized by crazed window-dressers), but the place positively effervesces and the stripped-down menu yields several solid hits. The Caesar salad is so richly dressed — sans tableside antics — as to constitute a meal. Move on, nonetheless, to a pair of lobster cannelloni slathered with tomato *coulis* — every bite fresh and light. Return visits have proved the kitchen's talent with pasta; now if only they'd replace the truly uncomfortable chairs. **(617) 367-8405. Mon–Wed 11:30–10, Thur–Sat until 11, Sun 5–10. No reservations. Moderate to expensive. AE, MC, V.**

....

Bob the Chef's

604 Columbus Ave, Boston

B OB THE CHEF'S, Boston's "Home of Soul Food," is a cheery, spotless place where long-time-no-see regulars get kissed by waitresses wearing nurse-white uniforms. The clientele reflects the surrounding neighborhoods of Lower Roxbury and the South End. Suits and coveralls dine side by side in comfort. The food tends to be diner bland, but quantities are homestyle generous and generally of high quality. Steer clear of the "Bar-b-qued" spareribs, however: they're steamed, fatty, and coated in a sauce as mild as mother's milk. On the other hand, the popular Chef's Glorifried Chicken is grease free, crisp outside, and moist inside. Add salt and pepper and it's some of the best in the city. **(617) 247-9773. No bar. Mon–Sat 11–9. Closed Sun. Moderate. N.**

....

Boodles

**Back Bay Hilton,
40 Dalton St, Boston**

THERE ARE PEOPLE who have spent their entire lives in Boston, yet they've never heard of the Back Bay Hilton. But the BBH is home to Boodles, an appealing place that combines a faux English-hunting-lodge decor with a kitchen expert in the ways of the grill. The steaks are well aged, the seafood fresh, the accompaniments interesting, and if you like calf's liver as much as we do, you can overindulge in a Boodles' model the size of a small Buick. **(617) 236-1100. Breakfast Mon–Sun 7–10:30. Lunch Mon–Sat 11:30–2:30. Dinner Sun–Fri 5–11, Sat until 11:30. Expensive. Cr.**

....

Café Calypso

578 Tremont St, Boston

OUR INITIAL assessment still holds: we should be so lucky as to have the Café Calypso in our neighborhood. It's such a pleasant place, with thriving plant life and the air of a permanent party. Where so few kitchens display a basic grasp of herbal properties, this one demonstrates genius. Fresh oregano brings out the best in a frittatalike pouf of *pancetta* and eggplant; saffron mayonnaise adds grace to the oven-poached blackfish. For haute finesse at café prices, this little South End storefront may well be the best deal in town. **(617) 267-7228. Beer and wine. Lunch Mon–Sat 11:30–2:30. Dinner Mon–Thur 6–10, Fri–Sat until 11. Sun brunch 11–3. No reservations. Moderate to expensive. MC, V.**

....

Cafe Sushi

**1105 Massachusetts Ave,
Cambridge**

CAFE SUSHI has become a Cambridge fixture, a kind of clubhouse conducive to communal delectation. We always overorder: several rounds of à la carte sashimi to tide us over till the chef's own selection arrives; a side of rich, briny *hiziki* seaweed; a dozen or so delicate, translucent forcemeat dumplings. Specials have included nouvellishly fanned slices of duck, with a sauce that somehow replicates the taste of pecans and cream. Finally, a place where raw-fish fanatics and finicky Europeanists can amicably co-dine! **(617) 492-0434. Beer and wine. Lunch daily 12–2:30. Dinner Sun–Thur 5:30–10, Fri–Sat until 11. No reservations. Moderate to expensive. MC, V.**

Cajun Yankee

**1193 Cambridge St,
Cambridge**

THE CROWDS have eased somewhat, but we're happy to report that the quality of cuisine at Cajun Yankee is not suffering in the least from postcelebrity slump. Junior bankers and superannuated students still willingly share tables to partake of generous platters of the fried crab claws and delights such as the heavily garlicked linguine with shrimp. The gumbo is spicy and authentic, the blackened redfish way above average. Desserts are daunting: the sweet-potato pecan pie would fuel a field hand, but the *crème Chantilly* topping — no Reddi-Wip here

— is a touch of pure Acadian class. **(617) 576-1971. Beer and wine. Tue–Sat 6–10. Closed Sun–Mon. Reservations recommended. Expensive. N.**

....

Cao Palace
137 Brighton Ave, Allston

C AO PALACE verges on being the ideal neighborhood spot. Go there when you're starving — there are a bunch of great dishes you mustn't miss. But don't go when you're faint with hunger, because the crowds linger forever in this funky Allston fish-market restaurant and the service is, uh, unhurried. This rub aside, the spanking-fresh fish and occasional pork and beef dolled up in sweet, spicy Vietnamese sauces are luscious. Simply following the rapidly accelerating punkification of Mr. Cao's kids (the, uh, unhurried waiters) makes repeat trips thoroughly worthwhile. **(617) 783-2340. Mon–Wed 12–10, Thur–Sat until 11. BYO. No reservations. Moderate. N.**

....

Changsho
1712 Massachusetts Ave, Cambridge

F ROM THE OUTSIDE it looks like a poured-concrete block; once inside, you'd swear you'd strayed into the oriental wing at the MFA. Changsho is a Chinese restaurant such as Cambridge has never seen — here a painted screen, there a primitive totem of fiber art, everywhere wooden columns with minimalist metal capitals. Nor is the art confined to the decor: every dish, from garlicky house soup to giant prawns and a sadistically spiced red pepper lamb, is delicate and fresh. For a spectacular finish, try the honey apple fritters, which arrive piping hot to be caramelized tableside in ice water. **(617) 547-6565. Sun–Thur 11:30–10:30, Fri–Sat until 11:30. Dim sum Sat–Sun 11:30–3. Reservations recommended. Moderate to expensive. AE, MC, V.**

....

Chef Chandler

329 Columbus Ave, Boston

PAST THE BAR SIGN at Tim's Tavern thanking you for NOT BREATHING WHILE I SMOKE is the small backroom domain of Chef Chandler, a refreshing razzberry to the blackened you–name-it cliché that has become Cajun cuisine. True, the BMW-ers who wait for a dinner table are spit-and-polish next to the bar denizens of this South End saloon, but all pretension is lost amid the cluttered decor and the verve of the staff. Willard Chandler, veteran of Boston soul kitchens, dishes up such marvels as roast chicken with oyster stuffing and gingersnap gravy, conch-and-seafood-creole pie, gumbo with mussels and lobster, and peach bread–pudding with bourbon sauce — and you'll carry home a doggie bag heavier than bayou mud. **(617) 247-7894. Dinner Mon–Sat 5:30–10. Closed Sun. Moderate. N.**

....

Chez Nous

147 Huron Ave, Cambridge

OUR DEFINITION of the civilized evening? Well-bred food, soft light, fresh flowers, and a corner table at Chez Nous. The chef-owner has overcome a small room, neighborhood location, and limited menu to create a restaurant that matches the best in downtown dining. The theme is usually French but essentially comes from the "with" school, as in duck with figs or smoked bluefish with plums. It may sound a bit precious, but there's nothing overly cute about the cooking, which is first-rate. The menu is rewritten daily, reflecting a dedication to only the freshest ingredients. Make reservations on weekends, or you'll have to take your red pepper soup and grilled tuna elsewhere. **(617) 864-6670. Beer and wine. Tue–Sat 6–10. Closed Sun–Mon. Reservations recommended. Expensive. AE, MC, V.**

The Colony

384 Boylston St, Boston

ACCOUTERED like a private club set about with brass and boating prints, The Colony attracts a self-select coterie of connoisseurs. They welcome the chance to see Bruce Frankel (also of Panache) not only do his stuff but explain it. Frankel's ideal these days is to apply European flair to transform native fare: hence a seafood stew like bouillabaisse infused with heady hard cider, or a fork-tender breast of pheasant ringed with pungent chunks of braised quince. We may not be California, but Frankel proves New England can be almost as rich a larder. The room's mood is still a bit studious, but artistry of this level can't help but elicit irrepressible pleasures. **(617) 536–8500. Tue–Sat 6–10. Reservations required. Very expensive. AE, MC, V.**

The Commonwealth Grille

111 Dartmouth St, Boston

THE COMMONWEALTH GRILLE is a fabulous-*looking* restaurant — from its mottled pink walls accented in bright turquoise to its leopard-patterned carpeting. The first time we visited, we took a seat at the bar, ordered white wine spritzers and a couple of tiny, trendy pizzas sprinkled with Montrachet, and watched the patrons play "Dahling, it's mahvelous to see you." We had fun counting courtships. The second time we stayed for dinner, and the pretentions were harder to digest. Perhaps the pork loin saturated with apricot sauce was just a poor choice, but we could think of no excuse for the pallid pesto that accompanied an exquisitely bland roast lamb. The desserts were uninspired, but these guys do a pretty nice roast potato. **(617) 353–0160. Lunch Mon–Fri 11:30–3. Dinner Sun–Thur 6–10:30, Fri–Sat until 11. Sun brunch 11:30–3. Café menu until 1 a.m. Reservations recommended. Moderate to expensive. AE, MC, V.**

Cornucopia

15 West St, Boston

I F YOU WANT pretty, Cornucopia's got it: pretty food, pretty chairs, pretty lamps, pretty people. Luckily, pretty here doesn't mean precious. The menu speaks nouvelle, but in a heartier voice: pork sautéed in applejack, cream, and syrup; grilled lamb on a bed of mustard-herb fettucine; a spectacular roast duck salad drizzled with herbed vinegar and laid out on chicory. The New American menu changes every month and hardly ever misses. Better yet, the spirit of the place isn't precious either — people actually look as though they're having *fun*. **(617) 338-4600. Lunch Mon–Fri 11:30–2. Dinner Tue–Sat 6–10:15. Reservations recommended. Expensive. Cr.**

Cranebrook Tea Room

Tremont St, South Carver

T HE Cranebrook Tea Room could be in an Agatha Christie novel, but this post-and-beam roadhouse by a pond is too good to leave to inquisitive ladies with their minds on murder. Calf's liver with onions in Madeira sauce was a savory turn on a homely dish. And the seafood crêpe bursting with succulent mollusks put the proof in the pudding — Cranebrook is way off the beaten track but certainly worth the mileage. **(617) 866-3235. Lunch Tue–Fri 11:30–3, Sat–Sun until 2. Dinner Wed–Sat 6–9:30, Sun 5:30–8:30. Reservations recommended. Expensive. MC, V.**

Daily Catch

323 Hanover St, Boston

As THE OLD Sicilian saying goes, you can bake, fry, or stuff it, but no matter, squash is always squash. One might say the same for squid, but not to patrons of the Daily Catch, a five-table, family-in-the-kitchen, kitchen-in-the-dining-room sort of place where you can't get too much calamari. Here the cephalopod is imaginatively marinated, scampied, sauced, even turned into meatballs. There's also pasta blackened with squid ink, a decidedly overhyped dish treated here as casually as one could hope. **(617) 523-8567. Beer and wine. Daily 12–10. Moderate to expensive. N.**

Dover Sea Grille

1223 Beacon St, Brookline

At THE Dover Sea Grille, the fish is broiled and the chips are mesquite. Potatoes are new; preparations are nouvelle (or Cajun). Hold the cole slaw and tartar sauce. The tuna comes with tomato–rosemary butter, the monkfish with chopped vegetables, and nothing comes cheap — except, perhaps, the person responsible for apportioning the blackened swordfish. The same person, no doubt, who in this otherwise elegant room sets the tables with paper placemats. **(617) 566-7000. Lunch Mon–Fri 11:30–2:30. Dinner Mon–Sat 5–10:30, Sun until 9:30. Sun brunch 11:30–2:30. Reservations recommended. Expensive. Cr.**

Durgin-Park

340 Faneuil Hall Marketplace, Boston

DURGIN-PARK, "established before you were born," remains an idiosyncratic monument to democratic Americana. With its low ceilings, yellow walls, communal tables, clatter of plates, and roaring crowd, it really is more dining room than restaurant. Everybody loves the raw clams and oysters (ask for horseradish and Tabasco), the huge beef and fish portions, and lobster. Meals are served with good, chewy cornbread and potatoes; the baked beans aren't bad, but the salad is pathetic. Genuinely gruff waitresses will bring *their* choice of dessert (Indian pudding, apple pandowdy) if they're out of yours. Stupendous at lunch, this is a venerable joint, the last rose amid the ferns of Quincy Market. As for the satellite branch at Copley Place — stay away. **(617) 227-2038. Mon–Thur 11:30–10, Fri–Sat until 11, Sun 12–9. No reservations. Moderate to expensive. N.**

L'Espalier

30 Gloucester St, Boston

OKAY, so it's a little stuffy. We take that back: what with the dim lights and the hushed tones and the hovering, tuxedoed waiters, L'Espalier is a *lot* stuffy. Now, normally this would bother us. But good food covers a multitude of pretensions, and the food here isn't just good, it's spectacular. The menu is inventive, yet nothing is done simply for the sake of being different. The sauté of mallard duck, for instance, was just *made* for maple vinegar sauce. If we hadn't worried about sounding like hicks, we would have asked for seconds on the chocolate sorbet. No quibble over the $50 prix fixe — worth every penny — but the wines are somewhat overpriced. **(617) 262-3023. Jackets. Mon–Thur 6–9:30, Fri–Sat until 10. Reservations required. Very expensive. Cr.**

Felicia's

145A Richmond St, Boston

BOB HOPE likes it hot. Luciano Pavarotti prefers his cold. Frank Perdue wants the recipe. It's Felicia's Chicken Verdicchio, a combination of chicken breast, button mushrooms, and artichoke hearts actually worthy of the menu hype. When you've tired of the precious pinkness of new-wave eating, this is the place to come: large rooms, family-sized tables, friendly waiters, and a lasagna *verde* that's big enough for two. **(617) 523-9885. Beer and wine. Dinner Mon–Tue 4:45–9:30, Wed–Thur until 10, Fri–Sat 4:30–10:30, Sun 2–9:30. No reservations. Moderate to expensive. AE, CB, DC.**

The Forest Cafe

1682 Massachusetts Ave, Cambridge

THE FOREST CAFE, an ancient bar on the edge of Harvard Square, serves up the most intriguing Mexican food you'll find in a city too often afflicted with the tidy concoctions of prep-Mex. These recipes are mostly originals and mainly delicious; the Sunday special of *puerco adobo* is a gem of pork tenderloin snappy with orange and cilantro. Everything's energetic and full of surprises (pumpkin seeds, coriander, peanut-and-chile sauce). At last: Mexican food in Boston that's more Oaxaca than Taco Bell. **(617) 661-1634. Dinner Wed–Mon 5–11. Closed Tue. Moderate. AE.**

Grill 23

161 Berkeley St, Boston

T HIS MAN'S MAN of a restaurant draws a heavy advertising and media business to its space in the lobby of the old Salada Tea Company building. Where mammoth Corinthian columns once supported Salada's vision of empire, today these columns decorate a handsome room in which steaks, chops, and expertly grilled fish fuel the attending hard drivers for the competitive afternoon ahead. **(617) 542-2255. Jackets. Lunch Mon–Fri 12–2:30. Dinner Sun–Thur 6–10:30, Fri–Sat until 11. Sun brunch 11–3. Reservations recommended. Expensive. Cr.**

Gyuhama of Japan

827 Boylston St, Boston

A T GYUHAMA OF JAPAN, both the eye and the palate are treated with aesthetic sensitivity. The lively sushi bar turns out impeccable sashimi and sushi, artfully clustered on large platters and à la carte trays. The cooked fare is presented with equal care: tempura arrives in a conical mound, and *ebisu* (cold shrimp in tangy sauce) are deveined and split for chopsticks. Even the tomato wedges in the tossed salad are arranged in neat circles. With Japanese restaurants becoming as common as Toyotas these days, Gyuhama's attention to detail sends it well ahead of the pack. **(617) 437-0188. Lunch Tue–Sat 12–2:30. Dinner Tue–Sat 5:30–11, Sun 5–10. Closed Mon. Moderate. Cr.**

Hartwell House

94 Hartwell Ave, Lexington

C LEARLY INTENDED to capture some of the high-tech trade in this neck of the Lexington woods, Hartwell House is so brand-spanking-new, it hurts: they've polished up the brass so carefully, you could go blind finding your way to the main dining room (modeled, so we're told, on the executive digs at Paramount Studios). Fortunately, this fervor has found its way into the food. An entrée of sweetbreads *en croustade* is quite expertly prepared, and desserts are as masterful as portions are minuscule. The place itself is the type of restaurant that impresses grandparents; still, we can't fault the cuisine. **(617) 862-5111. Lunch Mon–Fri 11:30–2:30. Dinner Mon–Sat 5:30–10, Sun 12–5. Reservations recommended. Very expensive. AE, DC, MC, V.**

Harvest

44 Brattle St, Cambridge

SUCH IS THE tweed-and-twaddle quotient at Harvest that you'd swear Harvard had endowed a chair in Applied Gourmetics. The food, like the company, is intelligent if a tad self-important: in a decade's worth of monthly menus we've never encountered a total clunker (the closest was a white chocolate cheesecake, an unfortunate case of bland-on-bland). The freshly prepared pasta is always superlative, as are the salads, fish, and game, all perennially tending toward the trendy. The Marimekko look may have long since cashed in its cachet, but this prototypical restaurant continues to hold its own. **(617) 492-1115. Lunch Mon–Fri 11:30–2:30. Dinner Sun–Thur 6–11, Fri–Sat until 11:30. Brunch Sat–Sun 12–3. Reservations recommended. Expensive to very expensive. Cr.**

....

Harvard Street Grill

398 Harvard St, Brookline

THE HARVARD STREET GRILL is a welcome addition to Brookline's short list of worthy restaurants. Ambitious without being pretentious, the room has the spare, clean, casual look of California. From the open kitchen the chef sends out a mixture of upscale ethnic, like spunky Thai shrimp with fettucine, and nouvelle standards (grilled tuna has become the hamburger of the eighties). Much as we hate to recommend chicken wings, the version presented here, marinated with oranges and fresh ginger, is simply the best. **(617) 734-9834. Beer and wine. Dinner Tue–Sun 5–10, Fri–Sat until 11. Sun brunch 11–3. Closed Mon. Moderate. MC, V.**

Jacob Wirth

31–37 Stuart St, Boston

FOR 119 years, Jacob Wirth has been serving the most authentic German food in Boston. At this cavernous restaurant, you can sit and be served traditional boiled meats from spareribs to pigs' knuckles on a bed of sauerkraut with an expertly boiled, skin-on potato — and wash it down with dark beer. **(617) 338-8586. Daily 11–11. Moderate. Cr.**

Julien

Hotel Meridien,
250 Franklin St, Boston

FLAGSHIP OF THE sumptuous Hotel Meridien, Julien continues to be an admirable pacifist in the culinary wars, nobly eschewing both the overcaloried armaments of Escoffier and the precious little pellets of the nouvelle poseurs. What one finds here, simply, is some of Boston's finest food, superbly prepared and handsomely presented. When the chef deploys a port-based sauce, he doesn't reduce it *ad absurdum;* when he offers salmon, he avoids tarting it up with whatever bad idea has recently proceeded from some Californian's heat-oppressed brain. The menu, responsibly small, may stand a bit right-of-center in the politics of gastronomy, yet it achieves remarkable variety and always offers something imaginative, demanding, even daring. **(617) 451-1900. Jackets. Lunch Mon–Fri 12–2. Dinner Sun–Fri 6–10, Sat until 10:30. Reservations recommended. Very expensive. Cr.**

....

Karoun

839 Washington St, Newtonville

KAROUN BEGAN in a modest Back Bay basement, then moved upstairs and west to a Newton facility that looks like a carnival pavilion. The menu offers a kebab-dominated glimpse into Armenian cuisine. *Karoun* means spring, so go ahead and spring for a fixed-price, multicourse dinner — it's a chance to have a succulent kebab and a sampling of dishes, such as stuffed zucchini and grape leaves, that might be fatiguing to consume in main-course quantities. On weekends expect crowds. **(617) 964-3400. Lunch Mon–Fri 11:30–2:30. Dinner Mon–Thur 5–10, Fri–Sat until 11. Closed Sun. Middle Eastern band performs Fri and Sat at 8:30; belly dancer at 9:45. Reservations recommended. Expensive. AE, DC, MC, V.**

....

Lai Lai

700 Massachusetts Ave, Cambridge

WE CONFESS to getting a bit jaded on the restaurant circuit — tired of Thai, crowded by Cajun. But then Lai Lai, dedicated to the ascendancy of Chinese seafood, got us moving again. Bring a gang to this one. The place can handle a party, and eating en masse will spare you a painful process of menu triage. Otherwise, you'll have to decide between peppery jumbo shrimp, sautéed mussels with ginger and garlic, and six kinds of squid. **(617) 876-7000. Sun–Thur 12–10, Fri–Sat until 11. Moderate. Cr.**

....

Legal Sea Foods

**5 Cambridge Center
(Main St), Cambridge**

SOMEONE in the White House must have good taste. Legal Sea Foods' chowder — included in the last two inaugural banquets — is indeed unsurpassable: tawny, sweet, and packing bivalves by the truckload. But something of a stockyard aura prevails, unfortunately, at the spiffy flagship restaurant in Kendall Square, where an imperious PA system rides herd over the patient waiting hordes. The management is laying odds you won't mind once you've reeled in a tender little broiled coho salmon, or some garlicky shrimp aswim in a sea of butter. They're right; you won't. **(617) 864-3400. Mon–Sat 11:30–10, Sun from 4. No reservations. Moderate to expensive. Cr.**

....

Locke-Ober

3 Winter Pl, Boston

ONE DAY, slogging through the financial district in vain search of a CD that wouldn't self-destruct, we decided to soften the pain of pitiful yields with supper at Locke-

Ober. After all, this institution has withstood every market wiggle for the last 111 years, and although the food may be no great shakes, the clublike ambience is as comforting as money in the bank. Mahogany dripping with ormolu, a clientele given to modulated murmurs, waiters who glide by in shin-grazing aprons: these are the verities we put stock in. Never mind that the sweetbreads *à la financière* arrive in a curdled, cornstarchy gravy — the Indian pudding is unsurpassable, with layers of flavor that trickle down like a windfall of Franklins. **(617) 542-1340. Mon–Thur 11:30–10, Fri–Sat until 10:30, Sun 5–10. Reservations recommended. Very expensive. AE, DC, MC, V.**

Le Marquis de Lafayette

**The Lafayette Hotel
1 Ave de Lafayette, Boston**

C ALL US DENSE, but we never really *got* nouvelle until Le Marquis de Lafayette showed the way: with flavors so true and clear, a taste is all it takes. Consider a *millefeuille* of salmon flecked with almond slivers or tenderloin of venison flanked by a fanned poached pear, its tiny green leaves intact. Sounds precious? It was an absolute treasure. Still, we've seen the Marquis's process taken to excess, as when it offered an all-lobster meal, from first course to last. **(617) 451-2600. Lunch Mon–Fri 12–2:30. Dinner Mon–Sat 6–10:30. Closed Sun. Reservations recommended. Very expensive. Cr.**

Matsu-ya

1790 Massachusetts Ave,
Cambridge

MATSU-YA MAINTAINS such a low profile — its privacy protected by rice-paper panels — that we'd walked by it for years, thinking it perennially closed. Then one day we actually tried the door, entered, and found the place packed: something tells us Korean could prove next season's Cajun. Among the reasons: an aesthetic tendency that renders sushi as no mere seaweed rolls, but oceanic bouquets, combined with an affinity for rough-hewn comfort food like hearty seafood stews and a lightly herbed tempura. The setting is your basic scarlet vinyl and Formica, but the waitresses are uniformly charming. We can't wait to make further forays into this fascinating but deceptively nondescript menu. **(617) 491-5091. Sun–Thur 5–10, Fri–Sat until 11. Moderate. MC, V.**

Michela's

245 First St, Cambridge

THIS MUST BE the new Kendall Square, all right. Enter an atrium decked with giant Roman parasols, and you've arrived at Michela's, whose *nuova cucina* campaign promise is "No red sauce" — at least not the kind you can find in a jar. The lamb arrives in a rich, ruddy, *chasseur*-style reduction, flanked by surprisingly elegant leek fritters on twin beds of pureed red bell pepper. It's a study in scarlet, all the more dramatic in a setting modeled on Carrara marble: off-white, putty, and pink. If only every woman in the room didn't out-svelte Christie Brinkley — it quite puts us off the megacaloric marvel that is *tirami su*. **(617) 494-5419. Lunch Mon–Fri 12–2:30. Dinner Mon–Wed 6–10, Thur–Sat until 10:30. Reservations recommended. Expensive. Cr.**

....

New Korea

1281 Cambridge St, Cambridge

IT SURE DOESN'T look like much, the New Korea, with its red vinyl booths and harsh white walls. So why is it usually packed? Word is out, that's why: the squid is spicier than Thai, the dumplings tastier than Peking's. Raw beef, marinated and tossed with rice and veggies, exemplifies this extremely friendly restaurant's commitment to the revival of tired palates. The Japanese would do well to worry, and not only about import tariffs. **(617) 876-6182. Mon–Fri 5–10, Sat–Sun from 12. Reservations recommended. Moderate. AE, MC, V.**

....

Ocean Club

The Charles Hotel Charles Sq, Cambridge

THE OCEAN CLUB has the curious appeal of a precocious adolescent: gawky pretention tempered by a clear desire to please. But the cooking does more than please, it dazzles with simple artistry. Mussels, for instance, may arrive in a lovely bisquelike stew suffused with saffron and Madeira; the clam pizzas (red or white) are so agreeably chewy, you'd better plan on a tussle and order at least two. Service is of the laid-back school — which provides plenty of time to observe a mating scene that has become Cambridge ritual. **(617) 576–0605. Lunch Mon–Fri 12–3. Dinner daily 6–12. Expensive. AE, MC, V.**

....

L'Osteria

109 Salem St, Boston

L'OSTERIA is a sunny throwback to times when local Italian restaurants were small and served great food at reasonable prices. This place has an obvious intent to please, from its eagle-eyed produce-buying to chatty service and graceful presentation. While antipasti in some North End eateries sit on sideboards for hours on end, the just-cooked freshness of L'Osteria's offerings can't be praised enough. The clams in garlic-laden white sauce are oh-so-sweet; the calamari is fork tender and lightly stuffed with seasoned bread crumbs. This is North End dining at its best, with no pretensions. **(617) 723-7847. Beer and wine. Tue–Sun 11–11. Closed Mon. Moderate. MC, V.**

....

P. A. Seafood Restaurant

345 Somerville Ave, Somerville

THERE IS a loud and lively Portuguese silver anniversary party going on at the next table, and at P. A. Seafood Restaurant, it stands to reason: anybody who makes it through twenty-five years of marriage deserves a dinner as good as this. The huge buckets of P. A.'s six different Iberian seafood stews — some sweet and tangy, others peppery, all thick with mussels, scallops, shrimp, and half a lobster — are impeccably spiced and wonderful. Couples have been known to swoon over the *lomo de cerdo alentejana,* pork with clams in a heady sauce. Could this be the solution to the soaring divorce rate? **(617) 776-1557. Lunch Mon–Fri 11:30–2:30. Dinner daily 5–10:30. Reservations for six or more. Moderate. AE, MC, V.**

Panache

798 Main St, Cambridge

P ANACHE gives you a choice of only thirty-eight seats, eight appetizers, and eight entrées. But there's a better than fair chance that by picking one of each, you'll have as good a meal as can be had in all New England. After blissing out on peppered venison, we attacked our partner's exquisite baby pheasant as if it were Rome and we the Visigoths. Dessert? Two of us shared one of everything, lingered an hour, and then, forced by the coming morning's responsibilities (never by the pleasant waiters), we stumbled off into the Central Square night. This is a superb restaurant. **(617) 492-9500. Beer and wine. Dinner Tue–Sat 6–10. Closed Sun–Mon. Reservations recommended. Very expensive. AE, MC, V.**

Peacock Restaurant

5 Craigie Circle, Cambridge

I F THE Peacock Restaurant were not housed in an apartment-building basement a few blocks shy of Harvard Square, there'd be no ceiling to the prices that chef and co-owner Sue Small could command. As it is, those of us who dine out regularly have found a haven in this lovely room. Small's penchant for provincial French cuisine yields stunning dishes at astounding prices: the sole *suchet*, a fresh filet embracing scallop mousse, will set you back a mere eleven dollars; the tender venison (topped with cranberries broiled to bursting) costs only a few dollars more. Elegant, intimate, and patently underpriced — it's almost too good to be true, and certainly too good to miss. **(617) 661-4073. Dinner Tue–Thur 5:30–9:45, Fri–Sat until 10:45. Closed Sun–Mon. Reservations recommended. Expensive. MC, V.**

Rainbow

275 Washington St, Newton Corner

E VERY CIVILIZATION seems to leave behind some negligible artifact that sums up the story. But what will future archaeologists make of Rainbow's plastic "twig" chairs? Every effect in this ultratrendy eatery seems calculated and false, from the brass kettle-drum lamps to the Oz-like spear-fence entry. We don't like being manipulated. But we *do* like the Rainbow Rita (a red, white, and blue sno-cone) and the veal paprika with buttery spaetzle. Better still is the Volcano — a brownie-based boulder of homemade chocolate ice cream enrobed in solidified hot fudge and drizzled with white chocolate and butterscotch. Okay, so we'd sell our soul for it — bring on the plastic palm trees. **(617) 964-7300. Sun–Thur 11:30–11, Fri–Sat until 12:30. Moderate to expensive. Cr.**

....

Rarities

**The Charles Hotel,
1 Bennett St, Cambridge**

RARITIES, the Charles Hotel's restaurant *de luxe,* is decorated in velvet black, like a jeweler's tray. We were swept away by the sensuous gray flannel chairs and waves of waiters so felicitous we'd have gladly paid to have them serve us air. The seasonal entrées (ruffed grouse, for one) can be unevenly seasoned (too much pepper), but side dishes of bite-sized baby carrots and crunchy wild rice salvage the main event, and the chocolate pâté is a marvel. You leave feeling as if you've scored the Koh-i-noor: skilled service is the jewel in this restaurant's crown. **(617) 864-1200. Jackets. Dinner Sun–Thur 6–10, Fri–Sat until 11. Reservations recommended. Very expensive. Cr.**

....

Rebecca's

21 Charles St, Boston

IF ONLY Rebecca's wasn't so successful. The minimalist decor is always so terribly cluttered with Y-people clambering for a roost with a view; the wait at peak-load times can run sixty minutes on up. With that kind of temporal investment, we tend to get peevish, impervious even to mussels in leeks and cream or the fluffy blandishments of a Gâteau St. Honoré. Oh, for the days of obscure exclusivity — now it seems the only solution is to observe peculiar hours. **(617) 742-9747. Beer and wine. Breakfast Mon–Fri 7:30–10, Sat from 8. Lunch Mon–Sat 11:30–4. Dinner Sun–Mon 5–10, Tue–Sat until 12. Sun brunch 11–4. No reservations. Expensive. AE, MC, V.**

....

Restaurant Jasper

240 Commercial St, Boston

I N THE PAST we've had our problems with Jasper's, our expectations being as high as the prices. But we've struck gold on several recent visits. Especially charming: a serendipitous brace of partridge thighs hugging a mound of chestnut and herb-bread dressing and lamb like a living geode, expertly browned on the outside, yet roseate within. True, the portions here are tiny, but, at last, we've had our money's worth. **(617) 523-1126. Dinner Mon–Thur 6–10, Fri–Sat until 11. Reservations recommended. Very expensive. Cr.**

....

Ristorante Toscano

41 Charles St, Boston

T HE CONTRAST between Ristorante Toscano at night and during the day is as dramatic as . . . gold lamé and tweed. P.M., the mode is all pomp and pretention, with officious wait-

ers zipping about like fast-frame Pinoc-
chios. Come for lunch and the tempo is
pure *passeggiata,* as loose and leisurely as
a Florentine trattoria. This is the pace we
prefer; time enough to indulge in paper-
thin *carpaccio,* a plate of plump tortellini,
espresso, *crème caramel* . . . Why attempt
the cuisine if you can't adopt the life-
style? **(617) 723-4090. Lunch Mon–Sat 11:30–
2:30. Dinner Sun–Thur 5:30–10:30, Fri–Sat
until 11:30. Reservations recommended.
Moderate to expensive. AE.**

....

Ritz Bar

**The Ritz-Carlton,
15 Arlington St, Boston**

W HEN THE DOG BITES, when the
accountant must be visited,
is there really any other place
to lunch in Boston? If you seek not a
dining experience but simple surcease,
the Ritz Bar is *there* with the Higher
Blandness, a club sandwich the way they
used to make them on the *Twentieth
Century Limited,* or eggs Benedict aswim
in flawless hollandaise, or a modest crabmeat salad sprinkled with capers. The
house white wine is generally a Macon-
Lugny; nobody asks for a wine list. Service is friendly to all, and if you want a
martini your waiter will not inquire,
"Gin?" Arrive early (or very late) for a
window table with a view of the tangled
trees of the Public Garden. **(617) 536-5700.
Jackets. Lunch 12–2:30. Moderate to expensive. Cr.**

....

The Romagnoli's Table

353A Fanueil Hall, Boston

THE FOOD AT The Romagnoli's Table doesn't make the earth move, but it's simple, satisfying, and easy to like. Although the wine list stretches from Como to Calabria, we bow to frugality and choose the house. The zesty red is in just the right spirit for the lively pasta with peas and unsmoked bacon that passes the al dente test. Minestrone has a lightness that seems almost Japanese, and the salad is well seasoned — all enough to make us oblivious (momentarily) to the overcrowded palace of mammon we escaped upstairs in Quincy Market. **(617) 367-9114. Daily 11:30–10. Moderate to expensive. AE, DC, MC, V.**

....

St. Cloud

557 Tremont St, Boston

SENSING AN AUDIENCE, a fluffy femme in mink and combat boots strides toward the mob at the bar, dogged by a leathered trio, heavily moussed. They spill around St. Cloud, the South End block party that happens also to serve a delicate salmon in saffron beurre blanc, searching for cheeks to buss while Billie Holiday wails. This is trendy (flat grays, etched glass, rhinestoned waiters) to the max. The desserts alone justify the struggle for a table, the happy crowds are a bonus. **(617) 353-0202. Lunch Mon–Fri 11:30–3, Sat until 4. Dinner Tue–Fri 5–12, Sat from 6, Sun–Mon 5–10. Sun brunch 11:30–4. Expensive. Cr.**

....

Seasons

**Bostonian Hotel,
Blackstone St, Boston**

T HE OVERALL MOOD at Seasons is more Los Angeles than Boston, and new chef Bill Poirier may have a tough time outshining the innovative Lydia Shire (who's decamped for the West Coast). He seems to be playing it safe so far, judging from the winter menu (the *carte* changes quarterly) — lots of straight grills and a salad of "field lettuce." There is a rebel yearning to cut loose, however: witness the tiny tributary of red pepper oil that lurks beneath the otherwise ordinary scallop dumplings. **(617) 523-3600. Breakfast Mon–Fri 7–10:30, Sat until 12, Sun until 11. Lunch Mon–Fri 11:30–2:30, Sat 12–3. Dinner Mon–Thur 6–10, Fri–Sat until 11, Sun until 9. Reservations recommended. Very expensive. Cr.**

Skipjack's Seafood Emporium

2 Brookline Pl, Brookline

W HY IS IT that Skipjack's Seafood Emporium feels contrived and impersonal, sort of like a yuppie theme park? Probably because of the obligatory Cajun appetizers (this year's nachos), the dashed-off *Miami Vice* decor (isn't that in reruns yet?), the chatty menu (enough already!), and the prepster waitrons (are you sure this isn't Harvard Square?). Too bad, because Skipjack's handles seafood just fine: the fish is fresh and carefully done, the crabcakes are plump, and the grilled redfish spectacular. If it weren't so damned self-conscious, Skipjack's might give that

Other Fish House a run for its money. **(617) 232-8887. Mon–Thur 11–10, Fri–Sat until 11, Sun 12–9. Reservations weekdays for six or more. Moderate. AE, MC, V.**

....

29 Newbury

29 Newbury St, Boston

THE DIFFERENCES between 29 Newbury and all the other chic eateries nearby are subtle but significant. This is discreet punk for the bourgeoisie. Start with the walls — not pink but a cozy terra-cotta. Cajun gets a nod, inevitably, but the homage is appropriate: tasso, for instance, lends bursts of Slim Jim bluster to a delicate dish of mussels and chive angel-hair pasta. Desserts have an irresistible aura, as in a cake of crushed macadamia nuts and white chocolate. **(617) 536-0290. Lunch Mon–Sat 11:30–3. Dinner Mon–Tue 5:30–11, Wed–Sat until 12. Sun brunch 12–11. Expensive. AE, MC, V.**

....

The Water's Edge

Congress St, Museum Wharf, Boston

YOU'D EXPECT The Water's Edge, a barge moored beside the Children's Museum, to collect the hyperactive spillover. But instead it's a sea of business suits, and the reason quickly becomes apparent: what better place to talk shop than this sumptuous wood-on-white setting with picture-window harbor views? The food is fairly serious, too: cold pasta with generous slathers of pesto and scallops so fresh they seem ephemeral. The homemade ice cream might easily inspire acts of piracy. **(617) 350-6001. Lunch Mon–Sat 11:30–3:30. Dinner Mon–Thur 6–9, Fri–Sat until 10; bar until 2 a.m. Closed Sun. Expensive. AE, DC, MC, V.**

....

White Rainbow

65 Main St, Gloucester

"To ADD another hue unto the rainbow," quoth the bard, "is wasteful and ridiculous excess." Dinner at the White Rainbow, however, seems an eminently sensible way to study the subtleties of the senses. The setting is Early American minimalist (one wall consists of massive blocks of granite), and the cuisine is progressive without being precious. Consider, for example, the veal *homard* (lobster-topped) in a celestial sauce of *crème fraîche,* brandy, and truffles. One taste, and the soul soars. **(617) 281-0017. Dinner Tue–Fri 5:30–9:30, Sat 6–10. Closed Sun–Mon. Reservations recommended. Expensive. Cr.**

....

The Wild Goose

300 Faneuil Hall Marketplace, Boston

Here we have fine-to-exciting dining in a slouchy enough setting to make Cantabrigians feel uncompromised by a trip across the Charles. No accident: this is the Faneuil Hall outpost of that fashionable Harvard Square feedbag, the enduringly vivid Harvest. An inspired menu emphasizing grilled game yields such trophies as pasta with oysters and white truffles and a worthy breast of goose in maple-pecan sauce (although the venison has been tamed to tastelessness). Said to be the first mesquite-fueled local grill, The Wild Goose has gone to gas — a gesture of reverse one-upmanship more than economy, we suspect, since at these prices they could afford mahogany chips. **(617) 227-9660. Lunch Mon–Fri 11:30–2:30. Dinner Sun–Thur 6–10:30, Fri–Sat until 11. Sun brunch 12–2:30. Reservations recommended. Very expensive. Cr.**

J OAN McNEAR of **Acacienne** (formerly Dom's of Needham, 238 Highland Ave, Needham) could give the downtown Northern Italian honchos some stiff competition . . . **Il Dolce Momento** (30 Charles St) serves the best gelato west of Florence . . . **Café China** (1245 Cambridge St, Cambridge) brings French style to eastern ingredients, and elegance to the province of cardboard-cartons-to-go . . . **TEC — Fast Food** (downstairs at 237B Newbury St) serves up little sea jewels of sushi, cafeteria-style, and cheap . . . For Indian we favor **Haveli** (1250 Cambridge St, Cambridge): the setting's prettier than most, and the seasoning's anything but hackneyed . . . The red curry shrimp at **Thai House** (1033 Commonwealth Ave) is the best in the city . . . **Rosemary** (623 Main St, Cambridge) is for noshing, French country-style: intriguing salads, enticing desserts . . . For nibbles, drinks, and the sublime Dave McKenna on piano, the **Plaza Bar** (at the Copley Plaza, Copley Square) . . . Breakfast? The **Ritz** (15 Arlington St), of course.

Worcester

MESQUITE has moved to Worcester, and its smoky-sweet aroma is now greeting guests at Gill's Grill, an enthusiastic eatery that serves the standards — shrimp, chicken, and sirloin — with style. Those with less pallid palates might try the sautéed skate wings or marinated squid. The clientele fills three art deco dining rooms to capacity on weekends, creating a noise level reminiscent of the Chicago Commodities Exchange. **(617) 366-7993. Mon–Sat 11:15 a.m.–11:30 p.m., Sun 12–10:30. Expensive. AE, DC, MC, V.**

Gill's Grill

157 Turnpike Rd, Westboro

FOOD PREJUDICES ABOUND. If yours include the belief that every meal requires meat, potatoes, and a green vegetable, best skip Keepers II. This place lavishes attention on dazzling

Keepers II

587 Bolten St (Rte 85), Marlboro

theatrical decor and a cutesy eighteen-page menu that lists legions of hot and cold appetizers, soups, salads, hamburgers, and Tex-Mex specialties. You could probably nosh yourself to death here, with a little hummus for starters, maybe a do-it-yourself thick pastrami sandwich for sharing, and certainly a generous wedge of double-chocolate cake to hoard. Cheerful, quick service encourages consumption, but the beautiful presentation invites restraint. **(617) 481-5353. No jeans after 5. Mon–Thur 11:30–10, Fri–Sat until 11. Closed Sun. No reservations. Moderate. AE, CB, DC.**

....

Legal Sea Foods

1 Exchange Pl, Worcester

SEAFOOD MAVENS find the weekly menus at Legal reassuring; for such freshness they willingly battle large, cheerful crowds crammed cheek-by-fin around the bar and tables downstairs. Upstairs is more decorous but less fun, since you can't peer at other diners' plates and appraise their choices. Food comes as soon as it's ready and servings are generous, so feel free to sample your partner's squid while you wait for your scrod. All the fish is wonderful, the staff cheerful, and, for the merely adequate side dishes, forgiveness is easy. **(617) 792-1600. Mon–Thur 11–10, Fri until 11, Sat 12–11, Sun 1–10. No reservations weekends. Expensive. Cr.**

....

Maxwell Silverman's Toolhouse

25 Union St, Worcester

AXWELL Silverman's Toolhouse is in the basement of a converted factory, and no one ever lets you forget it. For one mad moment, after they've brought the menu inside a wooden tap-and-die box, you worry that they just might carve the prime rib on a lathe. If you can ignore the blue-collar cutesiness, there's a suitable selection of steak and seafood to savor, including duck *bigarade* that's as crisp as promised. Service is quick and helpful. If you avoid the disco hours, which begin at 10, the setting encourages relaxed conversation and numerous after-dinner coffees. **(617) 755-1200. No jeans on weekends. Lunch Mon–Sat 11:30–2:30. Dinner Mon–Sat 5–10, Sun 4–9:30. Sun brunch 11:30–2:30. Expensive. AE, DC, MC, V, house charge.**

El Morocco

100 Wall St, Worcester

L MOROCCO is a family-owned restaurant with an unembarrassed heart. One night we heard three different renditions of "Happy Birthday," all played by a pianist who beamed as if each recipient were a cousin. Diners make their way down a list of Middle Eastern favorites, including fish satisfyingly smothered with onions, walnuts, and tahini and classic stuffed grape leaves. Weekend crowds are a drawback. To avoid being relegated to the dreaded Green Room on a packed Saturday, try a weeknight dinner. **(617) 756-7117. Lunch Mon–Fri 11:30–4. Dinner Mon–Thur 5–10, Fri–Sat until 11:30, Sun 4–10. Moderate. AE, MC, V.**

Struck Cafe

415 Chandler St, Worcester

RENOVATIONS can be risky, so the Struck Cafe had best beware. Born as an eccentric little place filled with personality and mismatched chairs, it has been muddling toward decorator mediocrity. Even the menu is growing sadly one-sided. On our last visit, almost every dish was doused with fruit. But don't take us wrong; the cooking is still great. Sole with nectarines and blueberries is excellent, as is the veal with lemon marmalade. But it's disconcerting to see a passion for fruit quite so unbridled. **(617) 757-1670. Lunch Tue–Fri 11:30–3. Dinner Tue–Thur 5–9, Fri–Sat until 10. Closed Sun–Mon. Reservations recommended. Expensive. AE, MC, V.**

Victorian House

16 Maple Ave, Ashburnham

THE VICTORIAN HOUSE is straight out of Mary Poppins, with a tall mansard roof and cheerful waitresses in severe black uniforms with crisp white caps and aprons. This family-run restaurant is eminently satisfying. Setting and service are gracious, and the menu offers a variety of complex dishes, beautifully cooked and fetchingly presented. Chicken *piccarde* arrives, garnished with melon balls, cranberries, and bright vegetables, on an ironstone plate. **(617) 827-5646. Wed–Sat 5–9:30. Closed Sun–Tue. Reservations recommended. Expensive. MC, V.**

....

S TURBRIDGE has never suffered from an identity crisis. The town fancies itself a slice of living history, and The Whistling Swan is no exception. The dining rooms are cozy and low-ceilinged and the wallpaper is period reproduction, as are the drapes, the paintings, and the oil lamps. However, the menu strays from Pilgrim rectitude with elegant decadence, offering a fine fettucine carbonara, frogs' legs Provençal, and swordfish *au poivre* that is blessedly underdone. There isn't a baked bean in the house. **(617) 347-2321. Lunch Tue–Sat 11:30–2:30. Dinner Tue–Sat 5–9:30, Sun 12–8. Closed Mon. Reservations recommended. Expensive. Cr.**

....

The Whistling Swan

502 Main St, Sturbridge

W HAT HAS little Petersham ever done to deserve a restaurant as good as The White Pillars? Separate dining rooms offer three different environments linked by the same glorious menu. The silky butternut bisque and tangy shrimp *dijonnaise* are memorable selections, and the service is warm and leisurely. On viewing the

The White Pillars

Rte 32 (on the common), Petersham

lushly decorated rooms for overnight guests upstairs, you'll be sorely tempted to move in — permanently. **(617) 724–3443. Dinner Tue–Sat 6–9, Sun from 2. Sun brunch 11:30–2. Closed Mon. Closed Jan–Feb. Reservations recommended. Moderate to expensive. MC, V.**

....

W HEN IT'S 5 A.M. and you're hungry, head for the **Boulevard Diner** (155 Shrewsbury St, Worcester) for a cheap, hearty meal served in one of the last of the great wooden diners . . . Try the excellent fried fish at **The Bar Lunch** (169 Main St, Hudson); disregard the seedy-looking facade and enjoy the food and chatter . . . **Cheng Du** (Rte 9, Westboro) may look like just another bland, shopping mall restaurant, but it offers serious Szechuan and Mandarin food of consistently high quality . . . When time is no issue, dine at **Arturo's Ristorante** (Fair Shopping Plaza, Rte 12, West Boylston); you'll wait forever but you'll learn why: the Northern Italian food is so good that no one wants to leave . . . For flamboyant celebrations, overlook the pretentiousness and enjoy the setting, the pampering, and the sometimes great food at **The Castle Restaurant** (1230 Main St, Leicester).

Pioneer Valley

A SHORT HISTORY of Beardsley's: in 1975, when it opened, the only facsimile of an edible meal in all Northampton. In 1984, when the rest of Main Street had succumbed to the invasion of the nouvellistes and the ethnicists, a beacon of solidity. In 1985, on several visits, the elegant presentation of such items as salmon scallops in port and lime sauce. And most recently, on an unexpectedly crowded Thursday, desperate service, watery espresso, an empty larder (all the specials were gone by eight o'clock), and five dinner companions who may never again trust our assertions that this place can be very, very good. **(413) 586-2699. Lunch Mon–Sat 11:30–2:30. Dinner daily 5:30–10. Sun brunch 10:30–3. Reservations recommended. Expensive. Cr.**

Beardsley's

140 Main St, Northampton

Carmelina's

9 Russell St (Rte 9), Hadley

THE FIRST TIME we noticed Carmelina's there was a line of people stretching from the parking lot to the dining room door. What's so compelling about a shabby restaurant with a tacky "Pasta 'n Veal" sign, we wondered. Silly us. Returning on an uncrowded weekday night, we tasted remarkable batter-fried pillows of mozzarella stuffed with anchovies and sun-dried tomatoes and succulent *Alfredo di Mare* — shrimp, scallops, and *real* crab in a joyously seasoned cream sauce. We understand the young chef learned his trade in Boston's North End. Tastes more like Rome to us. **(413) 584-8000. Dinner Tue–Sun 5–10. Closed Mon. No reservations. Moderate. Cr.**

La Cazuela

7 Old South St, Northampton

FOR A Mexican restaurant in New England, La Cazuela does pretty well. Although we're naturally suspicious of a menu that feels impelled to caution diners that "not all Mexican food is hot," judicious ordering can produce a lovely meal in this pleasant room, where the margaritas come very large, sufficiently fast, and suitably furious. Some rules: 1. Don't expect much from the garden-variety selection of appetizers. 2. Always choose the green tomatillo sauce over the red chili sauce. 3, 4, and 5. Count on the enchiladas, leap for the chilaquiles, and expect the service to be, well, laid back. **(413) 586-0400. Lunch Mon–Sat 11:30–2. Dinner Mon–Thur 5–9, Fri–Sat until 10, Sun 4–9. Moderate. AE, MC, V.**

....

The Depot

125A Pleasant St, Northampton

I F THE DEPOT had hit Northampton five years ago, it would have been a phenomenal success. But, restaurant-jaded as the town has become, one wonders. A soaring space carved from the city's old Richardsonesque train station, The Depot serves up a respectable sort of cuisine, a marriage of circa 1960 hotel (lotsa beef . . .) and 1980s food trends (. . . garnished with three-pepper butter). But maybe the management's not after Nouveau Northampton. The portions are large enough, and the desserts good enough, to make us suspect that its future rests with local undergraduates looking for a night out. **(413) 586-5366. Lunch Mon–Sat 11:30–2:30. Dinner Sun–Thur 5–9:30, Fri–Sat until 10:30. Sun brunch 11–3. Expensive. Cr.**

....

East Side Grill

19 Strong Ave, Northampton

A LTHOUGH we have in the past decried its bottled béarnaise, we find that when birthday lunches beckon or friends call to suggest a meal, the East Side Grill is ready. There is surely no better bar in town, as this one comes equipped with fresh oysters and cold boiled shrimp. The dining rooms are pleasantly appointed, the service warm, and the shrimp *étouffée* reason enough for us to hope that Cajun never goes out of style. **(413) 586-3347. Lunch Mon–Sat 11:30–3. Dinner Sun–Thur 5–10, Fri–Sat until 11. Moderate to expensive. AE, MC, V.**

The India House

45 State St, Northampton

L IKE MOST Indian restaurants, India House has little to recommend it by way of decor. The lights are too bright, the crowded dining room is too noisy, and the service is often abrupt. But there are evenings when we yearn to dip light wedges of poori into cool cucumbery *raita,* when we must have the chicken tandoori, flavorful and moist, when we can taste the heated curries even before we arrive at table. At times like this we hardly notice the lines, or the sometimes overambitious specials. **(413) 586-6344. Sun–Thur 5–9:30, Fri–Sat until 10:30. Moderate. MC, V.**

Marty's Riverside Restaurant and Bakery

4 State St, Shelburne Falls

L OVELY LITTLE time-warped Shelburne Falls now has a restaurant to suit its style: Marty's Riverside Restaurant and Bakery, overlooking the pre-Christo Bridge of Flowers. You could call the design Haute Hippie Provincial: Judith Russell's neo-naïf paintings deck the walls; the glass tumblers and goblets are hand-blown by Josh Simpson. The Mexican specialties are swell (including the homemade hot sauce), but sweets are the real draw here: tart cherry-rhubarb pie and a chocolate rum mousse for the memory book. **(413) 625-2570. Beer and wine. Tue–Sun 8 a.m.–10 p.m. Moderate. N, checks.**

....

Panda Garden

34 Pleasant St, Northampton

INSTITUTIONS of higher learning aside, the real indicator of a community's level of cultural attainment is how many first-rate Chinese restaurants it can sustain. In Northampton, Panda Garden may be less glamorous than Sze's, but it's sometimes better than the old standby in its imaginative menu. This is the place to go for seafood, for pork in black bean sauce, or for any of several red chili dishes. Skip the chicken specials, too many of which are relentlessly deep-fried. **(413) 584-3858. Mon–Thur 11:30–9:30, Fri–Sat until 11, Sun 2–9:30. Moderate. AE, MC, V.**

....

The Student Prince

8–14 Fort St, Springfield

THE ARCHETYPAL German restaurant, with beer steins on the wall and schnitzel on the menu, The Student Prince is comfortably authentic and confident in its Teutonic ambience. Opened in 1935, it resembles a jolly village, with bustling workers and signs of past ceremonies you're sorry you missed. We practically polka over the sumptuous tenderloin goulash and the sauerbraten served with spicy red cabbage (although the *Kassler Rippchen,* or smoked pork chops, sometimes lack the authentic zing). There's a fine selection of German beer and wine and a lively bar. The only things missing are the oompah band and the lederhosen — which, actually, is just as well. **(413) 734-7475. Mon–Sat 11 a.m.–12 p.m., Fri–Sat until 1 a.m., Sun 12–10. Reservations recommended. Moderate. Cr.**

Sze's

50 Main St, Northampton

COMPETITION around the corner, in the form of the upstart Panda Garden, seems only to have sharpened wits in the kitchen at Sze's, glorious Sze's. This doted-upon dining spot has an airy bar where patrons can while away the nearly inevitable Saturday night wait. A superior oriental menu is the attraction. The chef succeeds in offering a host of dishes multileveled enough to be the object of respectful, even passionate, discourse. Favorites include pan-fried dumplings, Governor's Chicken, and anything *mooshi* with a murky, evocative hoisin sauce. **(413) 586-5708. Lunch Mon–Sat 11:30–3. Dinner Sun–Thur 3–9:15, Fri–Sat until 10:45. Sun brunch 11:30–3. Reservations recommended. Moderate. Cr.**

FOR AFTER-THEATER DRINKS in Springfield, try **Cafe Manhattan** (301 Bridge St, Springfield), great bar, beveled glass, beautiful wood . . . We've always found the service slow, however willing the help at **Truc Orient Express** (1441 Main St, Springfield), but it's the valley's only Vietnamese restaurant, and pretty good at that . . . Lunch at **Jake's** (17 King St, Northampton), just opposite the Hampshire County Courthouse, and you'll find yourself in the company of half the lawyers in town and most of their clients; a funky place, serving decent burgers and consummate home fries . . . For breakfast, **Sylvester's** (111 Pleasant St, Northampton), named for former resident Sylvester Graham, inventor of the Graham cracker; everything home-baked is superb, especially the blueberry coffee cake . . . People frequent the **North Star Seafood Bar** (25 West St, Northampton) mostly for its late-night disco, but during the dinner hour this is the only place in town with sushi . . . And finally, the **Miss Florence Diner** (99 Main St, Florence), classic down to its counter stools; they have one hundred–odd items on their menu — none of them especially good, but all of them fun.

Berkshires

Gateways Inn Lenox

Café Lucia

90 Church St, Lenox

FOR LIGHT Italian suppers on warm mountain nights, consider the airy terraces of Café Lucia. A bottle of Soave Classico, a simple red-tipped lettuce and onion salad, and fresh Cape littlenecks in oil and garlic over linguine and you'll be reminiscing about late-night repasts on the Campo di Fiore. And after the Italian rum cake and espresso, you'll swear you hear strains of Respighi in the breezes rustling the Lenox pines. **(413) 637-2640. Lunch daily noon–2:30. Dinner Mon–Fri 5–10, Sat–Sun until 11. Sun brunch 10–3. Dec–Apr: dinner only Tue–Sat 5:30–9. Moderate. MC, V.**

Church Street Cafe

69 Church St, Lenox

YOU ARE LYING under stars at Tanglewood. Ozawa's interpretation of Handel is impeccable. You feel transcendent, having mixed your music with a fine preconcert meal at the Church Street Cafe. The food was light but tasty, especially the chicken sauté *basquaise* in its lovely shrimp, ham, white wine, and garlic sauce and the filet of sole in its tricky counterpoint of sweet peppers and chive butter. A truly satisfying overture. **(413) 637-2745. Lunch daily 11:30–3. Dinner Sun–Thur 5:30–10. Late-night menu Fri–Sat 10–11:30. Dec–Apr: lunch Mon–Sat 11:30–2:30; dinner Mon–Sat 5:30–9; closed Sun. Moderate. MC, V.**

Federal House

102 Main St (Rte 102), South Lee

L OCAL DINERS expect a lot of chef-owner Kenneth Almgren at the Federal House, and well-bred palates that haven't been spoiled by snazzy food trends are never disappointed. Every item, from the galantine of duckling in lingonberry sauce to veal scallops with mushrooms, is faultlessly prepared in the best European tradition. The dining rooms of this superbly appointed inn are certainly the most elegant in the area. **(413) 243-1824. Dinner Tue–Sun 5:30–9:30. Sun brunch 11:30–2:30. Closed Mon. Expensive. AE, DC, MC, V.**

Hancock Inn

Rte 43 (Main St), Hancock

J UST WHEN you think your search for an authentic Berkshire country inn is doomed by trendy renovations, you discover the Hancock Inn. It's as funky and out-of-the-way as Grandmother's house, complete with Victorian knickknacks and doors that don't quite fit. And the food, in a word, is yummy. The duck liver pâté on wild mushroom caps is as smooth as butter, the chicken breast stuffed with wild mushrooms and fresh herbs as close as there is to genuine regional cuisine. **(413) 738-5873. Dinner Wed–Mon 5–10. Closed Tue. Winter: closed Mon–Thur. Expensive. AE, MC, V, checks.**

Kim's Dragon Restaurant

1231 West Housatonic St, Pittsfield

THERE'S A testimonial on the menu of this Vietnamese restaurant supporting the local legend that Arlo Guthrie, who lives nearby, sponsored the establishment when its immigrant proprietors arrived here in the seventies. But regardless of its provenance, Kim's Dragon Restaurant is noteworthy mostly for the succulent Lemongrass Chicken, the peppery Shaking Beef, and a half-dozen lesser dishes of various oriental parentage. What's good here is terrific, and what's bad is something called Cá-Sòt-Cà. Don't ask: we warned you. **(413) 442-5594. Daily 5–10. Beer and wine. Inexpensive. N.**

Konkapot Kitchens

Main St, Mill River

KONKAPOT KITCHENS is difficult to find, and that's just fine with us. Once word gets out about its extraordinary menu, the lines will surely stretch all the way to the general store. Diners who master the twists and turns that wind to this sleepiest of Berkshire hamlets will enjoy such dishes as smoked sockeye salmon, grilled lobster with tarragon butter, and sole wrapped in a squash leaf and smoothed with sorrel sauce. Meats are smoked on the premises and grilled over sassafras and corn cobs; greens are home grown. All is served with grace and élan in a pleasant, converted village home. **(413) 229-6614. Dinner Tue–Sun 5:30–9:30. Sun brunch 11–4. Closed Mon. Reservations required. Moderate to expensive. MC, V, checks.**

Noodles

12 Railroad St, Great Barrington

YOU CAN TRACE Great Barrington's metamorphosis from a just-plain-folks South County burg to its present country-chic status by the eateries that have occupied this Railroad Street address. Only a few years ago it was Graham's, complete with pool table and an occasional brawl. Noodles is an entirely different kettle of fish — say, piquant Cajun swordfish grilled over mesquite. A variety of veal and fresh pasta dishes are all quite tasty and quickly prepared. The decor is nouvelle Boylston Street, but the prices are still small town. **(413) 528-3003. Lunch Mon–Sat 11:30–4. Dinner Sun–Thur 5–9, Fri–Sat until 10; espresso and desserts until 2 a.m. Sun brunch 11–3. No reservations. Inexpensive to moderate. MC, V.**

Paolo's Auberge

306 Pittsfield–Lenox Rd (Rte 7), Lenox

Paolo Eugster, the Swiss chef-owner of Paolo's Auberge, spent earlier seasons toiling, with considerable success, in the kichens at Wheatleigh. Now on his own, he's created a restaurant that would fit nicely on the shores of Lake Lucerne. The menu, like his homeland, is a pleasant mixture of French, German, and Italian influences and changes with the seasons. You may hear him in the kitchen, pounding the veal for schnitzel, but if you're feeling French, opt for a simple steak *au poivre* preceded by lobster bisque garnished with red and black caviar. An additional pleasure: the charming, white-linened front dining room. **(413) 637-2711. Dinner Sun–Thur 6–9:30, Fri–Sat 5:30–10. Sun brunch 11:30–2. Reservations recommended. Expensive. Cr.**

The Old Inn on the Green

Rte 57, New Marlborough Center

Let the record show that on a recent summer evening at The Old Inn on the Green, gastronomic perfection was achieved. It began with loin of pork served with lively honey mustard, built to succulent slices of duck breast in four-star Madeira and grape sauce, and climaxed with marvelous homemade rhubarb sherbet. The Old Inn is a 1760s landmark restored to its original simple splendor; the dining rooms are illuminated solely by candlelight. Prix-fixe dinners are served on weekends only; you can call ahead for the menu. **(413) 229-7924. Fri–Sun 5:30–9:30. Winter: Fri–Sat 6:30–9:30. Reservations required. Very expensive. N, checks.**

....

The Old Mill
Rte 23, South Egremont

I N AN ERA of creeping Ralph Laurenism, it's nice to find a place where the country colonial atmosphere grows out of the past and not out of a Manhattan daydream. The Old Mill is simple, warm, unself-conscious — as comfortable a spot to have dinner as you'll find in the Berkshires. Such lovely details as the stenciled plank floors don't shout for attention. The food, too, is sincere and generally quite good. Skip the routine calf's liver, but don't miss the delightful breast of chicken niçoise, and definitely allow yourself at least one chocolate dessert. **(413) 528-1421. June–Oct: Mon–Thur 5:30–9:30, Fri–Sat 5–10:30; closed Sun. Nov–May: closed Sun–Mon. Reservations recommended. Moderate. Cr.**

....

The Orchards
Rte 2, Williamstown

O N ROUTE 2, just across from the Grand Union, is The Orchards, a hotel and restaurant touted, by some bizarre stretch of the imagination, as a country inn. The peach stucco exterior with tinted windows suggests that the country in question is Saudi Arabia. Inside, however, it's pure nouveau Americana with all the grace

and charm of an Ethan Allen show-
room. Follow the bright lights and
you're in the dining room, where a des-
perately eager staff bounds about like
golden retriever puppies. By now, you
are fairly depressed by the prospect of
dining here, a mood not lightened by a
menu entry called Chicken Greylock.
But despair not. The food is sensational.
One hopes the ambience will mellow
but the chef won't change one iota. **(413)
458-9611. Breakfast Mon–Sat 7:30–10, Sun
from 8. Lunch 12–2. Dinner Sun–Thur 6–
8:30, Fri–Sat until 9. Reservations required.
Expensive. Cr.**

The Williamsville Inn

Rte 41, West Stockbridge

WE WERE RELIEVED a while back
when The Williamsville Inn
regained its senses and con-
signed a renegade chef to nouvelle pur-
gatory. Instead of facing gastronomic
minimalism, diners may once again
enjoy what the inn is traditionally
known for: generous portions of finely
seasoned fresh food amid simple and
gemütlich decor. A seasonal specialty,
tenderloin of veal scallops with chanterelles, is a consistently fine choice
when available. The service, even during that year of lapsed taste in the
kitchen, has always been charming. **(413)
274-6580. Mon–Thur 6–9, Fri from 5:30, Sat
5–9:30, Sun 5–9. Winter: closed Sun–Thur.
Reservations required. Expensive. MC, V.**

Y OU CAN PICK UP sushi-to-go, along with fresh pasta, at **Guido's Marketplace** (1020 South St, Pittsfield, Fridays– Sundays) or take your coffee, fresh-roasted, at **The Coffee Roasting Company** (177 Main St, Great Barrington) . . . High tea is served daily at **The Village Inn** (16 Church St, Lenox), and it's more than just orange pekoe — we're talking creamed mushrooms on toast, scones, trifle . . . For the high-end evening, check out the prix-fixe five-course dinner at the local Italian palazzo, **Wheatleigh** (West Hawthorne Rd, Lenox) . . . Amid all this uppie and yuppie splendor, leave us not forget our roots: there's still no better *real* food with *real* noise to go with it than the fare served at **Joe's Diner** (Center St, Lee).

Cape & Islands

Captain Linnell House

Skaket Rd, Orleans

PATTI PAGE's "Old Cape Cod" is captured at the Captain Linnell House, where preppies dine comfortably with dowager aunts and vacationing couples seek refuge from Hyannis's hoi polloi. There's no water view, but the garden, dominated by an old European linden and a majestic catalpa, is an offbeat counterpoint to the Cape's beaches. Service is appropriately formal. The menu offers creative combinations: poached sole and oysters in a delicate tomato sauce, or an appetizer of Wellfleet oysters, apples, and broccoli in a cream sauce. The chef surely has a spirit of adventure, but sometimes timidity with the seasonings leaves the diner yawning. **(617) 255-3400. Mon–Sat 5:30–9, Sun from 12. Reservations recommended. Expensive. Cr.**

Ciro and Sal's

4 Kiley Ct, Provincetown

THE BEST DESCRIPTION of Ciro and Sal's can be found in one of the many homespun poems plastered on its menu: "Down midsummer lane and cellar stairs to candled gloom and Sicilian airs." Chianti bottles are strung from the ceiling, and people here eat spaghetti the way pros do, spinning it on their spoons. The salad is just an excuse to eat the parmesan dumped on top. There are 104 items on the menu, including fifteen sauces for pasta and lots of *vitello* and *pesce*. You can top it all off with an authentic zabaglione. **(617) 487-9151. Dinner daily 6–11. Expensive. MC, V.**

Chanterelle

411 Main St, Yarmouthport

YOUR VACATION is almost over, it's been raining for thirteen days straight, and you're close to strangling your significant other. Now's the time to let Chanterelle soothe your savage breast with an ultracivilized meal. A lunch of plump salmon in a velouté of apricots and braised scallions, garnished with a fragrant orange blossom, can really make the sun come out. If that doesn't cheer you up, the strawberry tart will. On second thought, don't save this place to stave off disaster; it deserves to be savored on its own. **(617) 362-8195. Lunch Tue–Fri 11:30–2. Dinner Tue–Sun 5:30–10. Closed Mon. Reservations recommended. Very expensive. Cr.**

Cranberry Moose

43 Main St, Yarmouthport

BEFORE IT was the Cranberry Moose, it was the Cranberry Goose. A tony, contemporary restaurant set in a Colonial home, it's all white and brightly decorated with art posters. Small dining rooms and attentive service augment food carefully prepared with delicate herbs and unusual sauces, such as the appetizer of tea-smoked scallops with fiddleheads, and a portion of soft-shell crabs with Pommerey mustard, dry vermouth, jalapeño-pepper jelly, garlic, and butter. It's a pleasure to find a chef so willing to experiment, especially when the results are so appealing. Obviously, careful work goes into every aspect of the seasonally changing menu. **(617) 362-3501. Dinner 5:30–10. Reservations required. Very expensive. Cr.**

Jean's Country Cupboard

Main St, Harwichport

TOOLING AROUND Cape Cod in her sporty sky-blue coupe, Nancy Drew was constantly making pit stops at spots like Jean's Country Cupboard. In a sunny front parlor sparkling with corny curio glass, you can sit down to cranberry pancakes or an Egg McLou — same idea as the fast-food version except that the cheese is a recognizable dairy product, the ham a half-inch slab. **(617) 432-9232. BYO. Wed–Mon 7–2 and 5–9. Closed Tue. Inexpensive. N.**

McKeague's

220 Scranton Ave, Falmouth

S O THE ATMOSPHERE's a trifle ferny, and we're not particularly interested in yacht watching (having little regard for the RVs of the sea) — McKeague's, the café half of the Flying Bridge, is still an okay place to grab a bite. The service is snappy, the fish befittingly fresh, and the prices entirely reasonable. For $14 you can score a hefty wedge of swordfish, charred tic-tac-toe style at an open grill and topped with smoked-salmon butter — an intelligent interspecies pairing. The comes-with salad bar boasts a dill-flecked *insalata di riso* that would have passed as a pricey appetizer at a more sophisticated venue. **(617) 548-2700. Daily 11:30–10:30. No reservations. Moderate to expensive. AE, MC, V.**

Mews

359 Commercial St,
Provincetown

T HE MEWS has the double luck of being both sweetly tucked away and right on the waterfront. Years ago it served as a stable for horses used to carry oysters off the boats. Soft and pink, it provides all the right touches: bits of red lettuce in the salad, brown and wild rice laced with marjoram. The fresh littlenecks and the strawberry shortcake are the highlights of any meal here, and the servers are as efficient as blackjack dealers. **(617) 487-1500. Lunch Wed–Sat 11–3. Dinner Mon–Sun 6–1. Sun brunch 11–3. Expensive. Cr.**

Napi's

7 Freeman St, Provincetown

NAPI'S is a rarity in Provincetown: it's open year-round, and although it's an artists' hangout, there's not a wisp of pretense anywhere. What makes us return again and again is Napi's spectacular Pasta Portuguese. It arrives steaming with enough rounds of *lingüiça* — a cross between kielbasa and pepperoni — to play a game of checkers. **(617) 487-1145. Daily 8:30–10. Expensive. DC, MC, V.**

The Regatta

Scranton Ave, Falmouth

AT THE REGATTA, attention soon turns from waterfront vistas to the performance at table. This attractive eatery consistently produces some of the most creative cuisine on the Cape. Appetizers such as quail with wild rice duxelles and black fettucine with calamari spotlight Todd Scimeca's artistry. But save room for the grilled swordfish in creole sauce, and for dessert. Chocolate Seduction Cake with *sauce framboise* is better than a night with your favorite movie star. **(617) 548-5400. Dinner 5:30–10. Reservations recommended. Very expensive. AE, MC, V.**

Rose's

Black Flats Rd, Dennis

A TRADITION in the Cape town of Dennis for nearly forty years, Rose's is a homey place where the cooking makes no pretense at being cuisine. This is family-style eating, small

kids and grandmoms welcome. The restaurant offers a mix-and-match assortment of pasta, veal, chicken, steaks,
chops, and pizza. Success comes with
the pasta. The Fettucine Rosina in cream,
butter, and parmesan sauce is a Roman
fantasy, the lasagna is light with a robust
tomato sauce. The eggplant parmigiana
and the veal Marsala, though, are little
more than prosaic. **(617) 385-3003. Daily
5–10. Reservations recommended. Moderate. MC, V.**

....

AESOP'S TABLES (Main St, Wellfleet) is an all-around favorite: adventurous cooks and a marvelous bar tucked away on
the top floor, complete with cut-velvet fainting couches . . . **Cafe
Edwige** (Commercial St, Provincetown) does superior breakfasts:
homemade granola, fruit-laden waffles . . . Try the oysters baked in
breadcrumbs and cream at **The Impudent Oyster** (15 Chatham Bars
Ave, Chatham) . . . A giant among clam shacks: **Arnold's** (Rte 6,
Eastham).

Martha's Vineyard

Black Dog Tavern

**Beach Rd Ext,
Vineyard Haven**

IN VINEYARD HAVEN, you'd be hard-pressed to find a more nautical setting than the porch of the popular Black Dog Tavern. In winter, when the fireplace blazes, young and old gather round for hearty fare and friendly nattering. In summer, that year-round ambience makes it especially popular with off-islanders. Service is low-key and friendly, the food abundant and not gussied up. They serve a pretty good burger, and there's plenty on the menu for vegetarians. **(617) 693-9223. BYO. Breakfast Mon–Sat 6–11. Lunch 11:30–2:30. Dinner 5–9, Fri–Sun until 10. Sun brunch 7–1. Moderate. AE, CB, MC, V.**

Home Port

Basin Rd, Menemsha

HOME PORT is a local favorite in the up-island port of Menemsha, but that doesn't mean the management wants you to linger over your food. The lobsters and stuffed quahogs practically fly out of the kitchen. It's best to order the $21 platter: quahog, chicken lobster, french fries, and sweet bay scallops, as well as fried fish and oysters. The loaves of plain white bread that they slap on the table are good enough to steal. But please hurry. The crowd in front has reservations and you're sitting in their spot. **(617) 645-2679. Dinner 5–10. May–Columbus Day. Reservations required. Moderate. MC, V.**

....

Lambert's Cove Country Inn

Lambert's Cove Rd, West Tisbury

Lambert's Cove Country Inn invites you down a winding, woodsy midisland road. It's located in the former home of a bibliophile, and all the public rooms, including the dining room, are cozy and tastefully done up. The old-fashioned garden is a charmer for Sunday brunch or a preprandial drink. The fare is good if not distinguished, except for the chocolate mousse with Grand Marnier, an exceptional dessert. The setting is a delight you can't fill up on. **(617) 693-2298. BYO. Dinner daily 6–9. Sun brunch 10:30–2. Reservations required. Expensive. AE, MC, V.**

....

Ocean Club

Five Corners, Vineyard Haven

In an earlier life, the building that is now the Ocean Club was a service station, conveniently positioned at the busiest intersection in Vineyard Haven. You'd surely never know it except for a metal roof that makes dinner conversation reverberate around an otherwise elegantly appointed interior. More's the pity, for the sophisticated fare — manicotti stuffed with escarole and pine nuts, broiled salmon with tamari — begs for a more intimate locale. Given the summer crowds, dinners are more party than private affair. **(617) 693-4763. BYO. Dinner 5–11. Expensive. MC, V.**

The Wharf

6 Dock St, Edgartown

Although it's hard to believe, The Wharf was once a sweaty blacksmith's shop. Only the dark beams of this near-the-waterfront restaurant are a giveaway. The menu is simple and leans heavily toward fish: the tender fried squid rings and peppery clam chowder are particular favorites. The scrod sautéed in lime butter is flaky and delicate, but beware of smoked cod as rubbery as a Goodyear tire. **(617) 627-9966. Breakfast 8–11. Lunch 11:30–4:30. Dinner 5:30–10. Snacks 10–12. No reservations. Expensive. AE, MC, V.**

Patisserie Francaise (Main St, Vineyard Haven) serves wonderful omelettes, superb French bread . . . **Lawry's Fish Market and Restaurant** (Main St, Edgartown) is famous for no-frills lobster . . . **Feasts** (Chilmark) brings mesquite grilling up-island, and the fish love it . . . For drinks (and maybe a peek at Carly Simon), try the **Hot Tin Roof** (Airport, Edgartown).

Nantucket

THE Brotherhood of Thieves looks like an eighteenth-century dive — a suitable den for pickpockets, pirates, or L. L. Bean–style buccaneers. Once your eyes adjust to the candlelight, you can order up a grog and a bowl of robust chowder, or an overstuffed sandwich, accompanied by luscious shoestring french fries that could convert teenagers from McDonald's. We've also had a special of peppery lamb stew, simmered to symphonic harmony, and a carrot cake rich as gingerbread. Thieves are covertly committed to treating one another well, and that's what they do to you here. **No phone. Open about 11 a.m.–11 p.m. daily. Moderate. N.**

Brotherhood of Thieves

23 Broad St, Nantucket

EVERY SO OFTEN you encounter a meal so good as to erase all existential doubts. India House may sound like one of those quaint historic preserves where they expect you to worship the wainscoting, but don't pass it by. It's authentic all right, from the listing floors to the low-slung ceilings, but the cuisine is wave of the future. Get first crack at palatable Cajun: shrimp grilled in torrid spices but deglazed to delecta-

India House

37 India St, Nantucket

bility with beer. The house specialty, Lamb India, arrives as a tenderloin enrobed in rosemary-studded breading and cloaked with a vibrant béarnaise. How anything as plain as an apple can end up the apotheosis of pie is one of the many mysteries that make us regular celebrants. **(617) 228-9043. Breakfast Mon–Fri 8:30–10:30, Sat until 12, Sun until 2. Dinner daily at 7:00 and 9:15. Reservations required. Very expensive. MC, V.**

....

Jared's

**Jared Coffin House,
29 Broad St, Nantucket**

JARED'S DINNER MENU promises "appropriate starch," and the phrase somehow sums up the stuffiness that informs both ambience and cuisine. The ancestral portraits and nautical scenes that ring the formal room, and the fine seafood sausage cloaked in a smoky thermidorish sauce are above reproach. But the scallops are big and bland, and the salad dressing bottled. You'll fare much better in the hotel's rough-and-tumble Tap Room, with a platter called Pride of New England (codfish cake, brown bread, and exemplary baked beans) and desserts such as a deliciously gritty chocolate silk pie. **(617) 228-2405. Breakfast daily 8–11. Dinner daily 6:30–9. Closed Wed–Thur in May and June. Lunch in Tap Room. Reservations recommended for Jared's. Moderate (Tap Room) to expensive. AE, DC, MC, V.**

....

North Wharf Fish House

12 Cambridge St, Nantucket

ONE WOULD THINK that Nantucket Island, perched at the edge of the world's largest fishery, would have a flotilla of year-round restaurants with raw bars and menus devoted to fish. Not so. The North Wharf Fish House, tucked away at the end of Old North Wharf, is one of only a few places where off-season diners can enjoy the local bounty. Plump oysters and littlenecks with a good imported ale are an ideal summer marriage; in winter, the Fish House Chowder and stuffed quahogs are definitely worth trolling for. **(617) 228-5213. Beer and wine. Lunch 11:30–3. Dinner 6–10:30. Appetizers served all day. Moderate. AE, MC, V.**

The Second Story

1 South Beach St, Nantucket

THE RESTAURANT as a minor work of art: the stairs of the old townhouse leading up to The Second Story are action-painted, the dining room walls are sponge-printed, and the food is traditional layered with eclectic. Although sometimes it seems overdone, it is still done well, as in creamy artichoke-*chèvre* soup. The menu changes daily and tends (like the patrons) toward high spirits rather than haughtiness. The behind-the-scenes artistry makes this one of the best restaurants on the island. **(617) 228-3471. Dinner daily 7–9:30. Reservations required. Expensive. MC, V.**

21 Federal

21 Federal St, Nantucket

TWENTY-ONE FEDERAL is the kind of restaurant you wish you could pack up and take home. It boasts novelty aplenty, based on a solid foundation of culinary skill. We could list successful dishes ad infinitum, but consider this: grilled brace of quail with a lyrical sauce of reduced stock, port, and tangerines. Or this: delicate hand-made sweetbread ravioli, slathered in cream, chanterelles, and slivers of Smithfield ham. Or caramelized bread pudding, chestnut-cognac ice cream. Not to bore you, but it only gets better. The setting is superb, too — spare yet handsome rooms with well-spaced tables. **(617) 228-2121. Lunch Mon–Tue, Thur–Sat 11:30–2. Dinner Thur–Tue 6–9:30. Sun brunch 11:30–3. Closed Wed. Dinner only, during the summer. Reservations recommended. Very expensive. MC, V.**

FOR BREAKFAST, homemade blueberry muffins at **Downey Flake** (South Water St, Nantucket) . . . For big occasions, **Straight Wharf** (Straight Wharf, Nantucket), where each summer the chef does sinful things to salmon . . . For lobster, **The Nantucket Lobster Trap** (23 Washington St, Nantucket) . . . For pasta primavera, **DeMarco** (9 India St, Nantucket) — Italian passion in a Puritan package . . . For game, Nantucket-bred and boarding-school fancy, **Le Chanticleer** (40 New St, Siasconset).

Hartford

ONLY IN AMERICA can a former car wash grow up to be the most elegant restaurant in Hartford. At L'Américain, the name says it all: fine home-grown ingredients enhanced by nouvelle techniques. The atmosphere is private-club elegant, the service smooth, and the menu changes seasonally. Each time we visit, we're surprised not so much by the quality of the food but by the originality of each dish. Roast leg of lamb, for example, is served with a tart orange-cranberry sauce, and we wonder how we could have eaten it any other way. Desserts are paradise, but we wish they wouldn't overcook the brussels sprouts. **(203) 522-6500. Lunch Mon–Fri 11:30–2. Dinner Mon–Thur 6–9:30, Fri–Sat until 10. Closed Sun. Reservations recommended. Very expensive. Cr.**

L'Américain

2 Hartford Sq West, Hartford

Annie's Eatwell

98 Weston St, Hartford

ANNIE'S EATWELL, the burger joint of the 1980s as conceived by the folks who brought you tony L'Américain, is a relentlessly cheerful all-American family restaurant. The atmosphere is new-wave cute, with cherries on the walls and booths, banners hanging from the ceiling, and giant sculptures of pies and cookies adorning countertops. Food is new-wave serious: almost everything (shrimp, skewered beef, ribs, burgers, chicken) is grilled over hardwood or mesquite coals. Hand-formed, fat and juicy hamburgers are served on buns from Eatwell's own bakery. They can be had in thirteen different guises along with heavenly thin, crunchy onion rings that may turn your blood to Crisco. **(203) 525-1242. Sun–Thur 6 a.m.–9 p.m., Fri–Sat until 10. Beer and wine. No reservations. Inexpensive to moderate. Cr.**

Apricots

1593 Farmington Ave, Hartford

AT FIRST it all seems a bit too much. The name, the apricot-colored love seats, the pale-green walls adorned with hand-painted apricot trees. This is such a pretty place that it would probably continue to attract an upscale crowd even if it began serving meals in Styrofoam boxes. But don't be misled. This converted trolley barn perched along the Farmington River offers some of the freshest and most inventive cuisine in Connecticut, all of it served with quiet, elegant grace. Dinner brings one glorious dish after another: iced lobster garnished with dill, asparagus soup spiked with tarragon, chocolate-flecked Charlotte Russe. With food like this, who cares if the tables are small? **(203) 673-5405. Lunch Mon–Sat 11:30–2:30. Dinner Mon–Sat 6–10, Sun 5:30–9. Sun brunch 11:30–3. Reservations recommended. Expensive. Cr.**

....

Beijing Garden

**Loehmann's Plaza,
230 Farmington Ave,
Farmington**

DECORATED IN Chinese Modern, glass chandeliers, and warm brown everything else, the newly opened Beijing Garden makes a fresh statement about Szechuan, Hunan, and Mandarin cuisine. Here, the ubiquitous spring roll is pinky-sized and filled with egg and meat. The hot-and-sour soup emphasizes chicken and tofu, and the honey-colored Peking duck does not require special order and was deftly dissected at tableside. Service is fast and pleasant. **(203) 677-1110. Mon–Thur 11:30–9:30, Fri–Sat until 10:30, Sun 1:30–9:30. Moderate. AE, MC, V.**

....

Capitol Fish House

391 Main St, Hartford

IT USED TO BE that if you wanted to eat out in Hartford, you went to a political hangout masquerading as a restaurant, ordered veal parmigiana, and hoped for the best. But times are changing. Take Capitol Fish House: brick walls, potted palms, and polished oak booths offer casual downtown chic, and the menu offers seafood in all its glorious manifestations. All the standards are here, from the obligatory blackened redfish to baked scrod, and a lengthy list of daily specials includes more adventuresome fare such as brochette of mahimahi (dolphin fish). What's best is anything with linguine, especially creamy, luscious Pasta Neptune. **(203) 724-3370. Lunch Mon–Fri 11:30–2:30. Dinner Mon–Thur 5–10, Fri–Sat until 10:30. Closed Sun. Reservations recommended. Moderate to expensive. Cr.**

Carbone's

588 Franklin Ave, Hartford

WHEN EATING ITALIAN, we have our own rule of thumb: the bigger the peppermill, the more robust the fare. At Carbone's, the peppermill's a baseball bat. And the affable waiters wield it with glee, knowing the Veal Cuscinetto, an artichoked version of saltimbocca, won't wilt under the heady rain. Carbone's fried calamari is the best in town. The Shrimp Gaetano could be spicier, and the Caesar salad less drowned in dressing, but, oh, we carp. This is a place where you can find something increasingly rare: old, ethnic Hartford. **(203) 249-9646. Lunch Mon–Fri 11:30–2:30. Dinner Mon–Sat 5–10. Closed Sun. Moderate. Cr.**

Casa Portuguesa

1999 Park St, Hartford

Out of action for three years, Casa Portuguesa has reopened in its slightly seedy storefront neighborhood. We've returned again and again to sample what had been our favorite spot for good, inexpensive Mediterranean meals. Clams *a bolhao plato* are served in a garlicky brown sauce; the *paelha* is thick with lobster, shrimp, clams, and *lingüiça*. All of the above are washed down with generous glasses of *vinho verde*. But you really can't go home again, at least not at yesterday's prices. Alas, Casa Portuguesa is a bargain no longer. **(203) 233-3318. Lunch Tue–Fri 11:30–3. Dinner Tue–Wed 5–9, Thur–Sat until 10, Sun 12–9. Closed Mon. Moderate to expensive. MC, V.**

Cavey's

45 East Center St, Manchester

Our favorite Italian restaurant in the Hartford area happens also to be our favorite French restaurant. Cavey's, on the Manchester Strip, offers high-priced Italian upstairs, haute-priced French down below, and we can't fault either. The Italian venue is the larger, cheerfully accented with grand arching windows, antiques, and exposed brick. The linguine, abundant with clams, mussels, scallops, and shrimp in a wine-scented tomato sauce, is a particular favorite. But downstairs, amid quiet elegance while sampling sublime poached lobster with morels, we marvel at the sheer talent in the kitchen. These guys have created a country all their own — and we'll gladly apply for citizenship. **(203) 643-2751. Italian: Lunch Mon–Fri 11:30–2:30, Sat from noon. Dinner Mon–Thur 5–9, Fri until 10, Sat until 10:30. Closed Sun. French: Dinner Tue–Sat 6–10. Closed Sun–Mon. Reservations recommended. Expensive to very expensive. Cr.**

Congress Rotisserie

7 Maple Ave, Hartford

CONGRESS ROTISSERIE is done in minimalist black and white, and the food, which we first thought suspiciously trendy, is excellent. The place specializes in grilled salmon, chicken, and beef turned slowly on rotisseries in view of most tables. We love the goat-cheese and corn-cake appetizer, the Louisiana baby shrimp, and the succulent grilled salmon in a light sauce of tomato and basil. **(203) 560-1965. Mon–Thur 11 a.m.–1 a.m., Fri–Sat until 2 a.m., Sun 5–1 a.m. Reservations recommended. Moderate. AE, MC, V.**

Ficara's

438 Franklin Ave, Hartford

AFTER MUCH SEARCHING, Ficara's has emerged as our pick for fine dining on Franklin Avenue, Hartford's Little Italy. This tiny home *cum* ristorante produces *zuppa de pesce* that inspires a hearty chorus of "Torna A Sorrento." Veal ala Sebby (the house specialty) arrives on a huge platter draped with asparagus and cheese and awash with light sherry sauce. There's no liquor license, but you can bring your own wine. Frothy cappuccino is a nice finishing touch. **(203) 549-3238. Lunch Mon–Fri 11:30–2. Dinner Mon–Sat 5–10. Closed Sun. Reservations recommended. Moderate. MC, V.**

Flower Drum Song

798 Park Ave, Bloomfield

ENVY THE LUCKY FOLKS of Bloomfield whose neighborhood restaurant is Flower Drum Song: the talent in the kitchen is astonishing. Nothing beats a guided trip with local habitués, so listen up, Pilgrim, and take our menu advice. Skip the egg rolls and wonton soup. Head directly for hot-and-sour soup and pan-browned dumplings, followed by sesame shrimp (ask for it if it's not listed). Then go for sautéed string beans, General Tso's chicken, and pork with bean curd homestyle. Bingo. Welcome to the neighborhood. **(203) 243-5623. Mon–Thur 11:30–10, Fri–Sat until 10:30, Sun 4–9. Moderate. AE, MC, V.**

Gabriel's

Summit Hotel,
5 Constitution Plaza,
Hartford

THERE'S SOMETHING uncomfortably nouveau riche about Gabriel's, like a meat-and-potatoes man in a tux. The restaurant's affectations — roses for the ladies, sorbet between courses, warm hand towels after dinner — are amusing, but really, does the food require such diversionary tactics? It's a welcome surprise to find that the offerings, beef especially, rise above the pretentious folderol. Rosy, butter-tender beef Wellington, accompanied by nicely undercooked vegetables, wins a top rating. Gabriel's should stop blowing its own horn; this food can sing a cappella. **(203) 278-2000. Lunch Mon–Fri 12–2. Dinner Mon–Sat 6–11. Closed Sun. Reservations recommended. Expensive. Cr.**

The Hearthstone

678 Maple Ave, Hartford

THE HEARTHSTONE's new owners have pulled off quite a feat, re-opening this restaurant with much of its well-loved character intact while meeting eighties' expectations of food and ambience. The place looks great, with its dark, polished wood, deep red fabric, and etched glass (although we'd prefer *real* flowers on the table). While bowing to the new American cuisine, the kitchen still prepares the old classics best, and almost any piece of meat grilled on the fieldstone hearth will send you home happy. Despite the silly names, we especially like Steak à la Mike, with its powerful garlic kick, and Filet à la Moe, garnished with asparagus, lobster, and horseradish hollandaise. **(203) 246-8814. Lunch Mon–Fri 11:30–2:30. Dinner Mon–Thur 5–9:30, Fri–Sat until 10:30, Sun 4–8:30. Reservations recommended. Expensive. Cr.**

The Parson's Daughter

Main St and Hopewell Rd, South Glastonbury

THE Parson's Daughter has always been generous with beef, such as her rare medallions napped in traditional béarnaise. She sets a rather traditional table. Nothing too nouvelle here, as befits an old, rambling Colonial home: just quality food, well presented. The Caesar salad is prepared tableside, and the swordfish steak evolves into a world-class entrée when dotted with rosemary and sun-dried tomatoes. **(203) 633-8698. Jackets. Lunch Tue–Sat 11:30–2. Dinner Tue–Thur 5:30–9, Fri–Sat until 10. Sun brunch 11:30–3. Closed Mon. Reservations recommended. Expensive. Cr.**

Que Huong

355 New Park Ave, Hartford

THE VIETNAMESE restaurant Que Huong is in a borderline neighborhood, and its interior looks mostly like an H&R Block office — all flimsy paneling and vague attempts at low-budget decor. But the food is first class: *Bun Cha Geo,* crispy golden egg rolls on a bed of rice stick noodles, are a meal in themselves. *Ga Kho Dung* is hot, hot, hot, and the caramelized chicken breast with ginger overtones is a spectacular dish. Wash it down with bring-your-own beer and finish with an icy flan custard. **(203) 233-7402. No bar. Lunch Tue–Sun 11–2. Dinner Tue–Thur 5–9, Fri–Sat until 10. Closed Mon. Moderate. MC, V.**

Shenanigans

1 Gold St, Hartford

W HILE IT'S NOT exactly a garden paradise (the café tables are simply placed on a concrete sidewalk with no greenery in sight), at this point Shenanigans is the best place in Hartford for lunch in the sun, and a favorite late-night stop as well. A red, white, and blue motif greets you inside the restaurant, and a completely restored diner (circa 1946) contains the ever-busy bar. The chili is super: thick, two-alarm magic smothered in cheddar and spring onions. The salads — large, fresh, and original — are laced with crunchy green beans, sesame seeds, and interesting dressings. **(203) 522-4117. Breakfast Mon–Fri 7–10:30. Lunch Mon–Sat 11:30–2:30. Dinner daily 5:30–10; late-night menu 10–1. Sun brunch 11–2:30. Reservations recommended. Moderate. Cr.**

Tapas

1150 New Britain Ave, West Hartford

I MAGINE THE BEST mini-pizza you've ever had — that's tapas — at Tapas, an upscale Mediterranean restaurant where everything looks small and tastes fabulous. You can sample pies with sausage, Brie, mushrooms, and sun-dried tomatoes; with shrimp, artichoke, crab, and ricotta; and for dessert, with apples, almond amaretto butter, brown sugar, and cheddar. Wear jeans and be prepared to wait for a table. **(203) 521-4609. BYO. Mon–Wed 11:30–9, Thur–Sat 11:30–10, Sun 2–8. Inexpensive to moderate. N.**

W E'VE COME TO expect so little from Vietnamese restaurants in the way of decor that Truc Orient Express is a pleasant surprise. Bamboo tables and chairs in an airy glass enclosure may never be featured in *Architectural Digest,* but they do improve our disposition. We are further impressed with the food: egg rolls in an unusually light and crisp wrapper, and *moc,* a savory soup of chicken and black mushrooms, is delicious. *Banh Xeo,* described on the menu as a "happy pancake," is more like a crunchy fried turnover — oily but addictive. **(203) 249-2818. Lunch Tue–Sat 11–2. Dinner Tue–Sat 5–11, Sun–Mon 4–9. Reservations recommended. Moderate. Cr.**

Truc Orient Express

735 Wethersfield Ave, Hartford

....

S TOP IN AT STYLISH **Max on Main** (205 Main St, Hartford) to observe the wild life — can this be Hartford? — and to order "stone pie" (they used to call it pizza) . . . Before Bushnell events, **Lloyds** (60 Washington St, Hartford), where a trio will play Gershwin while you graze contentedly on a raft of diminutive dishes . . . For middle-of-the-night ice cream attacks: **Barnaby's** (831 Farmington Ave, West Hartford) . . . **Pacifico** (904 Farmington Ave, West Hartford) is the sort of place where you applaud the decor: Memphis comes to Hartford . . . For downtown lunches, **Municipal Restaurant** (455 Main St, Hartford) serves *real* hamburgers and a good cup of soup . . . **Jonathan's Park Cafe** (26 Trumbull St, Hartford) offers a late-night light menu and a soothing, plush decor ideal for after-theater.

Fairfield County

Apulia

70 North Main St, South Norwalk

FANS OF Maria's Trattoria will welcome Apulia, which has been opened across town by Maria's owners. The restaurant's up-to-date menu (radicchio comes to South Norwalk!) pairs pasta with the likes of salmon, fresh mozzarella, broccoli, and baby octopus. So close to and yet so far from the SoNo renovations, Apulia is an advance guard for culinary sophisticates. **(203) 852-1168. Lunch Mon–Fri 11:30–3. Dinner Mon–Thur 5–10, Fri–Sat until 11. Closed Sun. Reservations recommended. Expensive. Cr.**

Bloodroot

85 Ferris St, Bridgeport

THE FLAVOR OF THE early seventies persists in the seasonal vegetarian menu at Bloodroot, a feminist restaurant and bookstore. The homemade whole-grain breads and hearty soups, served in mismatched dishes you carry to wooden tables, recall the brash democracy of the Woodstock generation. The mood is mellow, the food is wholesome, and the dining room provides a pleasant view of the Sound. **(203) 576-9168. Beer and wine. Lunch Tue, Thur–Sat 11:30–2:30. Dinner Tue–Thur, Sun 6–9; Fri–Sat until 11. Sun brunch 11:30–2:30. Closed for dinner Mon and Wed. Moderate. N, checks.**

....

Café du Bec Fin

199 Sound Beach Ave, Old Greenwich

TASTE IS what makes the difference between innovation and outrage. It's also what makes Café du Bec Fin an exciting place to dine. While in step with nouvelle fashion, these folks realize that food is meant to be savored, not hung on the wall. The range-fed chicken is tenderly roasted and the *millefeuille* floats like a cloud over strawberries and cream. The espresso is served in cups more appropriate for a dollhouse. **(203) 637-4447. Lunch Tue–Fri 12–2. Dinner Mon–Thur 6:30–9, Fri–Sat 6–10. Reservations recommended. Expensive. AE, DC, MC, V, local checks.**

....

Chez Bach

43 Main St, Westport

CHEZ BACH offers the flakiest of spring rolls and faithfully reconstructed recipes from Madame Bach's native Vietnam. The surroundings are simple to the point of spare

— maybe even sparse. Food is the primary focus, and here it is elegant, custom-prepared, and exquisitely seasoned. True, a view of the Saugatuck River is a plus only at high tide, but this Westport branch of the original Branford restaurant maintains the high culinary standards that established Madame Bach's reputation years ago. **(203) 227-6586. Lunch Tue–Fri 11:30–2:30. Dinner Sun, Tue–Thur 5–10, Fri–Sat until 11. Closed Mon. Reservations recommended. Expensive. Cr.**

La Clé d'Or

8 Sconset Sq, Westport

I F YOU ARE in the mood for quiet European professionalism of the old school, La Clé d'Or fits the bill. The peaches and cream decor, crisp linens, and fresh flowers establish a formality that matches the cuisine. The quality of this small, elegant establishment is epitomized by the crusty, yielding French dinner rolls, exemplars of competence and tradition. This is not a sun-dried-tomato-and-goat-cheese emporium, but rather a place for silky smoked salmon, flawless sweetbreads, consummate *coquilles,* and tender filet mignon, all served and presented with the grace of an earlier time. **(203) 222-0770. Jackets. Dinner Mon–Thur 6–9:30, Fri–Sat until 10. Closed Sun. Reservations recommended. Very expensive. Cr.**

Le Coq Hardi

Big Shop Ln, Ridgefield

L E COQ HARDI is a fancy restaurant that curiously blends grotto decor (stone walls, dim lighting, few windows) with pink linen tablecloths, and a few stylized rooster figurines. The French-accented menu offers something for everyone with deep pockets, from an esoteric rabbit pâté suspended in aspic with kumquat compote to the more familiar rack of lamb with garlic and rosemary. Presentation here is decidedly nouvelle and the pretty plates arrive looking good enough to frame. For dessert, try anything chocolate. **(203) 431-3060. Jackets. Lunch Sun, Tue–Fri 12–2. Dinner Tue–Sat 6–9, Sun 5:30–8:30. Closed Mon. Reservations required. Very expensive. Cr.**

Hunan Garden Restaurant

330 Connecticut Ave, Norwalk

H UNAN GARDEN Restaurant follows the Fairfield County rule that no kitchen will ever take you seriously when you request dishes "very spicy." But it is an exception to the inconsistency of other area Chinese restaurants, where one visit is great and the next only so-so. Sun-Shein Wor Pa — a flavorful broth loaded with snow peas, shrimp, and chicken — is as warming as a ray of sunshine. And though we wish the chef would give it more kick, the Hunan Spicy Beef makes us very happy indeed. Service is unrushed but quietly attentive, and on Friday and

Saturday nights, there's a cocktail pianist after six. **(203) 866-3727. Mon–Thur 11:30–9:45, Fri–Sat until 10:45, Sun until 9:45. Moderate. AE, MC, V.**

....

Inn at Mill River

26 Mill River St, Stamford

L ITTLE DETAILS are immediate clues to the quietly courteous, cordial, and correct service you'll find at the Inn at Mill River. Your glass is kept magically full, the tables are luxuriously far apart, and the plush decor muffles sounds for an exquisitely quiet meal. Attention to detail shows in the food, too, from the artful arrangement of vegetables alongside a rosy rack of lamb to the ineffably combined sole and lobster *en croûte*. This is dining, first class. **(203) 325-1900. Jackets. Lunch Sun–Fri 12–2:30. Dinner Mon–Sat 6–10, Sun until 9. Reservations recommended. Very expensive. Cr.**

....

Maria's Trattoria

172 Main St, Norwalk

M ARIA'S TRATTORIA is the kind of intimate bistro you'd expect to stumble upon on a back street in Florence; to find it in a Norwalk storefront is just thrilling. You wonder how a place so small, scarcely more than a dozen closely packed tables, can support a menu this big and this good. Escarole soup, punctuated with tiny meatballs, is an excellent starter. All the familiar Italian specialities — ricotta-stuffed cannelloni, baked ziti, and the like — are prepared with delectable finesse. And your bill is testimony that there *are* a few bargains left in Fairfield County after all. **(203) 847-5166. Lunch Mon–Fri 11:30–3. Dinner Mon–Thur 5–10, Fri–Sat until 11. Closed Sun. Reservations weekdays only. Moderate. AE, DC, MC, V.**

....

Mesón Galicia

250 Westport Ave, Norwalk

I T'S REASON ENOUGH to go to Mesón Galicia simply to savor the aroma of the *pollo al ajillo* (sautéed chicken in garlic sauce) as it arrives bubbling hot and *muy picante*. The delicious *caldo gallego*, soup with greens and white beans, is typical of the lush, rainy northwest corner of Spain that gives its name to this inviting restaurant. But the menu features cuisine from all over Spain: Valencia's famed paella, spicy chorizo, Segovia-style lamb, hake à la Basque. Short of a ticket to Madrid, you couldn't ask for more. **(203) 846-0223. Lunch Mon–Fri 12–3. Dinner Sun–Thur 5–10, Fri–Sat until 11. Reservations required. Expensive. AE, DC, MC, V.**

....

Mr. Lee Szechuan Cuisine

64 Main St, New Canaan

T RUST New Canaanites to eat Szechuan in style. No Naugahyde booths or bordello wallpaper here — the look at Mr. Lee Szechuan Cuisine is strictly Breuer-chair chic. Even so, it's a comfortable family place, attracting quiche-fed young scions in Ralph Lauren rugby shirts or what passes for suburbo-punk. Dining *en famille* is a good way to sample several house specialties, such as the thirty-dollar dual-course Peking duck. Mr. Lee is famous for his Orange Beef. But the surprise hit is the unprepossessingly titled Crab in Brown Sauce, five or so sweet, batter-coated, garlicky crustaceans that one must unceremoniously suck one's way through (there's no way to save face). Mr. Lee even manages a spectacular send-off: Sesame Banana, a stuffed *beignet* sprinkled with red sugar. All very rich, to be sure. **(203) 966-3686. Lunch Mon–Sun 11:30–2:30. Dinner Mon–Thur 5–10, Fri–Sat until 10:30, Sun until 9:30. Reservations recommended. Expensive. Cr.**

Mulligan's Grill & Tap Room

183 Cherry St, New Canaan

WHILE IT'S TRUE New Canaan lacks the nautical ambience of, say, Rowayton, Mulligan's Grill & Tap Room still manages to serve the best bowl of steamers ever. They're tiny, grit-free, and traditionally accompanied by a cup of broth and a small ocean of melted butter. The mostly seafood dinner menu provides excellent and abundant fare, and the pub menu includes creditable burgers and other predictables. Most important, though, everybody's having fun. **(203) 966-3991.**

Lunch Mon–Sat 11:30–3. Dinner Sun–Thur 5–10, Fri–Sat until 11. Sunday brunch 11:30–3. Tap room menu daily 11:30–12. Reservations recommended. Moderate. Cr.

....

Paris Bistro

3546 Main St, Bridgeport

FORGET YOUR PIQUE over the anticlimactic return of Halley's comet and set your sights on the horizon's next rising star, Paris Bistro. The soft lighting is soothing and the service efficient, but what really has our mouths watering is the warm salad of sole and sweet sea scallops, arranged temptingly but not too preciously on a bed of endive and lettuce. After enjoying the pink-centered marinated sirloin in pepper sauce and an unusual first course of smoked chicken with lentils and red pepper strips, we're just glad we don't have to wait seventy-six years to return. **(203) 374-6093. Lunch Mon–Fri 11:30–2:30. Dinner Mon–Thur 6–9:30, Fri–Sat 5:30–10. Closed Sun. Reservations recommended. Expensive. AE, MC, V.**

....

The Peak

390 Post Rd, Darien

SOMETHING TELLS US this is not what Keats had in mind when he wrote, "Silent, upon a peak in Darien" — The Peak (yes, in Darien) is rather noisy for its small size. It's a congenial sort of clamor, though, and even if the out-of-season salad is not worth versifying, this is a fine spot for a Spanish-accented meal. The paella (enough for two or more) is made to order and well worth the forty-minute wait. In the meantime, you can pretend you're in Spain and enjoy the sharp and vinegary gazpacho. **(203) 655-7027. Lunch Mon–Fri 11:30–2:30. Dinner Mon–Thur 5–10, Fri–Sat until 11. Closed Sun. Reservations required for paella Fri–Sat. Expensive. Cr.**

Pasta Nostra

116 Washington St,
South Norwalk

PASTA NOSTRA offers homemade noodles and sauces — delicate, light, northern Italian — that are a triumph. The pesto here is so good it could regain its culinary ascendancy. Indeed, this is the sort of place that makes even dieters order appetizer and dessert. For the former, try the stuffed, roasted pepper; for the latter, don't miss the raspberry-chocolate cake, feather light and rich enough to cause hallucinations. Pasta Nostra is also a store (open Tue–Sat 10:30–6), selling much of its menu to go. **(203) 854-9700. Lunch Tue–Sat 11:45–2:45. Dinner Sat 6–10. Closed Mon. Moderate. N, checks.**

Restaurant Jean-Louis

61 Lewis St, Greenwich

CHEF EXTRAORDINAIRE Jean-Louis Gerin's first restaurant, Guy Savoy, closed after a small fire, but like a phoenix rising from the ashes, he has re-created his earlier triumph by opening the Restaurant Jean-Louis on the same site. A staunch supporter of American ingredients, Gerin uses fresh New York State foie gras in a variety of ways and floats medallions of lobster serenely in a coral sauce. If the restaurant has a flaw — the decor, service, and food presentation are impeccable — it may be in the somewhat esoteric menu. Sweetbreads in three different guises *is* a bit excessive. **(203) 622-8450. Lunch Mon–Fri 12–2. Dinner Mon–Fri 6:30–9, Sat 6:30 and 9:30 seatings. Closed Sun. Expensive. Cr.**

Sagres
250 Knowlton St, Bridgeport

FLAWLESS FRYING is an unusual and splendid thing. So is eating well in an honest-to-God, nongentrified urban neighborhood. Sagres gives you both. The tasty *mariscada* is brimming with clams, scallops, shrimp, and lobster and has just enough cayenne to flavor without burn. The fried whiting is delicate, crunchy outside, glistening white and flavorful within. You may need to call for directions and then inquire at a gas station or two, but persistence pays off. **(203) 334-4454. Daily 8 a.m.– 10 p.m. Moderate. N.**

Stick to Your Ribs
1785 Stratford Ave, Stratford

WHAT? Another barbecue joint? And in Stratford — and run by . . . an Englishman? Suspend your disbelief and drive to Stick to Your Ribs, off I-95 Exit 31 south, for the best Texas-style mesquite-grilled ribs, brisket, and sausage to be found between Aroostook and the Bronx. You can chow down in your car or at the outdoor picnic tables. This chef studied the best barbecue cuisine in Dallas, Houston, and Austin before throwing his first slab in the oven, and obviously he's learned his trade well. The place is clean, the pork exquisite. Calvin Trillin take note. **(203) 377-1752. Mon–Sat 10:30–9, Sun 12–7. No reservations. Inexpensive to moderate. N.**

Swanky Franks

182 Connecticut Ave, Norwalk

HEAVEN ON A BUN. What's left to be said? At Swanky Franks, hot dogs are served every which way, from stark naked to smothered in chili. The fries are hot, salty, and plentiful. And the onion rings are made fresh daily. You can see Swanky's from Exit 14 of I-95, which is just as it should be. **(203) 838-8969. Mon–Fri 10–9, Sat 10–7. Closed Sun. Inexpensive. N.**

Water Street

50 Water St, South Norwalk

WATER STREET is practically the cornerstone of South Norwalk's renaissance and serves the best food in the neighborhood. On a Friday night it's noisy (bar traffic!) and smoky, and the service can be slow, but the seafood, mostly creole in feeling, is well prepared and nicely seasoned.

There's gumbo to delight the Yankee soul — no okra — and scallops tender and sweet on angel-hair pasta. **(203) 854–9630. Lunch daily until 3. Dinner Tue–Sat 6–10, Sun from 5. Reservations recommended. Moderate. Cr.**

....

GOOD FOOD, ample portions, and palatable prices are encased in a slightly "ye olde" atmosphere at the **Redding Road House** (Rtes 53 and 107, West Redding), but the filet mignon and onion rings are superb . . . There's probably no Chinese food that isn't on the menu at the festive and frantic **Panda Pavilion** (1300 Post Rd, East Westport) . . . Indian food? **Mayur** (52 Sanford St, Fairfield) . . . For a decent burger and just plain good food, **Donovan's** (138 Washington St, South Norwalk) — the stalwart corner tavern that was an institution long before SoNo got groovy . . . **Perillo's Ristorante** (274 Connecticut Ave, Norwalk) has great garlic rolls and a cappuccino guaranteed to jolt.

New Haven

The Amber Restaurant

132 Middletown Ave,
North Haven

THE AMBER RESTAURANT, a.k.a. "The Place for Ribs," should also bill itself as the place for bar-becued chicken. Half a succulent bird is grilled until the skin is delicately charred, then bathed in the same tangy-sweet sauce that graces the ribs. Crisp onion loaf and garlicky slaw approach the Platonic ideal of the B-B-Q side dish. Takeout is available for those who dislike ersatz wood paneling and beer-logo clocks. **(203) 239-4072. Lunch Tue–Fri 11:30–2. Dinner Tue–Thur 4:30–9, Fri–Sat until 10, Sun 4–8. Closed Mon. Moderate. MC, V.**

Bruxelles Brasserie & Bar

220 College St, New Haven

THERE ARE NOW three theaters on College Street: The Palace, The Shubert, and Bruxelles Brasserie & Bar. The newest and smallest of the three is actually a hopping bistro with a decidedly stagy bent. The lustrous black-and-white set and cast of betoqued cooks shine beside the exposed rotisserie, but tables covered with butcher paper and appointed with a beaker of crayons approach absurdity. Food is often an afterthought in places like this, but Bruxelles does better than most, especially in the genre of light after-theater repasts. The thin, blistery, California-style pizzas are splendid, as are oversized salads and gooey desserts. But the main acts — remarkably uneventful plates of grilled poultry, beef, and fish — have let us down more than once. Choose carefully, and hope for a change of script. **(203) 777-7752. Sun–Thur 11:30 a.m.–midnight, Fri–Sat until 1 a.m. Moderate to expensive. AE, MC, V.**

Chavoya's

883 Whalley Ave, Westville

A T LAST A Mexican restaurant where the food is more than a follow-up to the margaritas. And whose spices earn, rather than burn, a place in your heart. Chavoya's sheds the Tex-Mex stereotype in other ways, too: an apricot and white, sombrero-free decor; an attentive but not sycophantic staff; and plate presentation Japanese-like in its artistry. We suggest you skip the enchilada-burrito-tostada offerings because there is so much more, including deftly turned seafood and tender, just-spicy-enough *carne tropical.* And the flan, as thick and smooth as ice cream, is now our paradigm. **(203) 389-4730. Sun–Thur 11 a.m.–10, Fri–Sat until 10:30. Expensive. AE, MC, V.**

....

Elm City Diner

1228 Chapel St, New Haven

T HE ELM CITY DINER doesn't specialize in Salisbury steak or waitresses wearing nursing uniforms. Here, vested servers, a smartly dressed crowd, and a baby grand stretch the diner concept considerably. So do entrées such as duck in apricot-almond sauce and cheese tortellini in scallop marinara. But this *is* the genuine article, a late-twenties, Mountainview model with a reputation for puffy onion rings that befits its humble origins. The menu covers a lot of ground: at one end are burgers, at the other are exuberant shellfish and pasta dishes. This erstwhile Formica classic would rather be true to taste than true to type — a laudable innovation, with no apologies to purists. **(203) 776-5050. Mon–Thur 11:30 a.m.–1 a.m., Fri until 2 a.m., Sat 11 a.m.–2 a.m., Sun 11 a.m.–1 a.m. Moderate to expensive. Cr.**

....

Hatsune

93 Whitney Ave (corner of Trumbull), New Haven

T HERE'S SOMETHING pleasantly untrendy about Hatsune, a minuscule, understated Japanese restaurant with a handsome bar, the kind where lemons, not raw fish, are sliced. Sushi and sashimi are available here, to be sure, but the emphasis is on farmhouse cuisine: charbroiled fish, shellfish, and meat, and huge, earthy stews served in cast-iron pots. Among entrées, a standout is *hokkai nabe,* an aromatic, gingery bouillabaisse in a bubbling miso broth. The chef favors a certain spice in all its permutations, as in nicely charred ginger pork medallions and delicate ginger cake. **(203) 776-3216. Lunch Mon–Sat 11:45–2:30. Dinner Mon–Thur 5–10, Fri–Sat until 11, Sun 4–9. Moderate to expensive. AE, MC, V.**

....

Jimmie's at Savin Rock
---
5 Rock St, West Haven

DON'T EXPECT any surprises when you visit Jimmie's at Savin Rock, a cavernous, glass-walled box of a restaurant anchored on Long Island Sound. Not unless you consider huge portions, real french fries, broiled-shellfish platters, and a flotilla of cheerful, competent waitresses to be surprises. If you're in an unpiscivorous mood, try the dish that was a mainstay back when Savin Rock was an amusement park and Jimmie's a hot dog stand. Split and grilled, Jimmie's dogs are still a wail ahead of the pack, and the waitresses won't flinch at the $1.40 order. **(203) 934-3212. Sun–Thur 11 a.m.–10, Fri–Sat until midnight. Inexpensive to moderate. MC, V.**

....

Miya Restaurant

1217 Chapel St, New Haven

TO PARTAKE of raw fish at Miya is to experience the essence of the East in its purest form. The waiters are patient tutors of your taste buds, explaining the difference between hand-formed and rice-rolled specialties, suggesting steamed seaweed for starters, and gently directing your attention away from the chicken and beef teriyaki. The *ebi,* tiny sweet shrimp, and *ikka,* squid enhanced with a mysterious mint herb, leave one feeling incredibly virtuous. The owner goes all out for her regulars and has been known to call a homesick compatriot when she's made spicy dumplings just like Mom's. **(203) 777-9760. BYO, tea only. Lunch Tue–Fri 12– 2:30. Dinner Tue–Thur 5:30–10:30, Fri–Sat until 11, Sun 5–10. Closed Mon. Moderate. N.**

Modern Apizza Ristorante

874 State St, New Haven

IF YOU'RE LOOKING for New Haven's famous Wooster Street pizza without the famous Wooster Street lines, Modern Apizza is the one for you. They've got the same brick ovens, the same crisp crust, the same fresh sauce that tastes like tomatoes rather than tomato paste, the same choice of toppings — but no waiting in line. Modern also has virtues of its own, like spinach and garlic pizza, an odd-sounding combo that, with its delicate texture and aroma, is closer to an elegant hors d'oeuvre than a simple peasant pie. Takeout available. **(203) 776-5306. Beer only. Open Tue–Thur 11 a.m.–midnight; Fri–Sat until 1 a.m.; Sun 3–11. Closed Mon. Inexpensive. N.**

....

The Orient

376 Elm St, New Haven

BECAUSE THE NAME doesn't end with *Gardens* or *Palace* and the slightly ramshackle decor has neither bamboo prints nor wind-chime light fixtures, you might guess that The Orient's food is out of the ordinary. And so it is. Dishes range from hauntingly delicate (cold broccoli with nutlike miso sauce) to richly assertive (fresh perch with ginger-lemon dressing) and downright fervent (Szechuan-style chicken and zucchini). Evidently the owners — he Chinese, she Japanese — know how to wed tradition with imagination, and the results are wonderfully unconventional. **(203) 777-3747. BYO. Dinner Sun–Thur 5–9, Fri–Sat until 10. Inexpensive to moderate. N.**

....

Peppino's

1500 Whalley Ave, New Haven

WAY OUT at the edge of Woodbridge, Peppino's is about as far from Wooster Square as a New Haven restaurant can be, but it'll hold its own against any Italian restaurant in town. Though its decor is rather a mishmash (stucco, hardwood, a few fake Tiffanies, a mounted swordfish), be assured there's no haphazardness in the kitchen. The smoky, filling soup of escarole and beans is the perfect remedy for somnolent taste buds, although it's dangerous to overindulge before the main course. Each of the full-flavored pasta entrées fills a bowl big enough to bathe a baby. Seafood combinations, such as calamari and shrimp over linguine, and scungilli and mussels on ziti, are particular standouts. The soft-shelled crabs are seasonal, but rival Baltimore's finest. **(203) 387-2504. Mon–Sat 11:30 a.m.–11, Sun 12–10. Moderate to expensive. AE, MC, V.**

....

Peter Cheng

177 Park St, New Haven

N O ONE who has been to Peter Cheng, not even takeout customers, expects to get out in under two and a half hours. With just one waitress and Cheng solo in the kitchen, dishes arrive one at a time, no matter how many you've ordered. Time-killing strategies include Scrabble, Trivial Pursuit, and reading the string of reviews posted on the otherwise blank walls, all written by people who concluded, as we always do, that the wait is worth it. His hot-and-sour soup, for example, appears with enough floating ingredients to be called a stew. **(203) 624-5913. Mon–Thur 5–9, Fri–Sat until 10. Closed Sun. Reservations recommended. Moderate to expensive. Cr.**

....

Robert Henry's

1032 Chapel St, New Haven

I F THIS were antebellum Atlanta, Scarlett O'Hara would dine at Robert Henry's. The place radiates old-fashioned opulence, with marble, mahogany, and etched glass. But the food doesn't languish in sentiment. The considerable imagination of the chefs delivers such beguiling inventions as cream of celery-root soup garnished with glazed chestnuts and steamed cod wrapped with leeks and infused with coriander. So what if the service is slightly unctuous? Frankly, my dear, with flavors like these, we don't give a damn. **(203) 789-1010. Lunch Mon–Fri 12–2. Dinner Mon–Thur 6–9:30, Fri–Sat until 10. Closed Sun. Very expensive. Cr.**

Sally's Pizza

237 Wooster St, New Haven

T HE SEARCH for the best mozzarella in this pizzaphilic city ends at Sally's, where the coal-fired brick oven yields crisp, flat ovals that stun the gustatory senses. Hot bricks give the crust its ashy tinge, and Salvatore Consiglio's special genius gives the sauces their authority. One taste of his *salsa bianca* and you may go tomatoless for life. The oblong, paneled room offers little to look at other than the oven's tantalizing produce, and you'll see lots of it before your moment comes. **(203) 624-5271. Beer only. Tue–Sat 5–12, Sun until 10. Closed Mon. Inexpensive. N.**

Serino's at Short Beach

126 Shore Dr (Rte 142),
Branford

T HE DECOR at Serino's reminds us of a finished basement, and the menu seems a routine discourse of standard Italian. But there's nothing routine about preparations that pair marinara and anchovy sauces on the fried mozzarella, *crème anglaise* and mixed-berry puree on the cheesecake. Those offerings that most restaurants botch through affectation — veal *Français,* for example — are executed with simple elegance. But the best moments come at the meal's two extremes — spectacular loaves of salt-tinged bread and a velvety *crème brûlée* that send us singing into the night. **(203) 481-6707. Beer and wine. Sun, Tue–Thur 5:30–9, Fri–Sat until 10. Closed Mon. Reservations recommended. Expensive. MC, V.**

A LTHOUGH WE USUALLY prefer the pies at Sally's or Modern, when we want white clam pizza we go to **Pepe's** (157 Wooster St, New Haven), despite the snippy service . . . **Tony and Lucille's** (127 Wooster St, New Haven) is the place for calzone, with three dozen fillings, from sausage to scungilli . . . At **Clark's Dairy Restaurant** (74 Whitney Ave, New Haven), you can still get a real brown cow from the soda fountain and homemade soups of the bean and barley persuasion . . . For the whole-wheat crowd, there's **Claire's Corner Copia** (1000 Chapel St, New Haven), where desserts are standouts (especially the Lithuanian coffee cake).

Southeastern Connecticut

ABBOTT'S Lobster in the Rough is as good as its name. Nothing fancy, just the kind of open-air seafood orgy one dreams about on cold winter nights: plastic plates, plastic bibs, picnic tables with a view of the Sound. Is there really any other way to eat a lobster? Plan to wait at least thirty minutes on weekend evenings. **(203) 536-7719. BYO. Thur–Tue 12–9 from Apr 30–Sept 27. Closed Wed. Moderate. MC, V.**

Abbott's Lobster in the Rough

117 Pearl St, Noank Village

WHOLE CLAM DINNER—is there anything else?" is how the regulars place their order. Although you'll find much more, you'll also come to understand their point of view. At The Clam Castle, scallops and fish are unrelentingly fresh, lightly battered, and fried to simple satisfaction;

The Clam Castle

1324 Boston Post Rd, Madison

hand-cut onion rings are firm and addictive. But, no doubt about it, plump and juicy whole clams (forget about *strips*) are the virtuosi, playing their parts with just enough crunch and more than enough ocean tang to turn tentative diners into mollusk mavens. This place is closer to a shack than a castle, but it needs a moat to keep the crowds away when nearby Hammonasset Beach is open. **(203) 245-4911. From Memorial Day to Labor Day Sun–Thur 7 a.m.–11 p.m., Fri–Sat until midnight. Winter hours Sun–Thur 7 a.m.–9 p.m., Fri–Sat until 10. Inexpensive. N, checks.**

Copper Beech Inn

Main St, Ivoryton

WE CONFESS that for a while the Copper Beech Inn wasn't our first choice for high-end dining: the fussy menu was more pomp than circumstance. But a new chef has made this inn a contender in any "best of " competition. Lissome crêpes with caviar and *crème fraîche* are only elegant previews to the main attraction, truffle-stuffed beef Wellington in a masterful Madeira sauce. The skill of the attentive staff, the napkins twisted artfully into spiked coronets, and the bounty of a blissful white chocolate mousse are among the marvels in this garden of earthly delights. **(203) 767-0330. Dinner Tue–Sat 5:30–9, Sun from 1. Closed Mon. Reservations recommended. Very expensive. Cr.**

Fiddlers Seafood Restaurant

4 Water St, Chester

I F YOU'RE UNSUCCESSFUL in your bid to weasel a table at Chester's Restaurant du Village, go instead to Fiddlers Seafood Restaurant, a little place off the main drag. Meticulously stenciled, the blue and winter-white dining room provides relaxed service and attention to culinary detail. The crusty spikes of garlic bread with aioli dip brace the palate, and the calamari are both crunchy and succulent in their marinara sauce. The *coquilles* Saint Jacques may prove unequal to the kitchen's high standards, but the white chocolate mousse with lingonberries will convince you that coming here as a second choice doesn't mean settling for second best. **(203) 526-3210. Lunch Tue–Sat 11:30–2. Dinner Tue–Thur 5:30–9, Fri–Sat until 10, Sun 4–9. Closed Mon. Reservations recommended. Moderate to expensive. CB, DC, MC, V.**

Fine Bouche

Main St, Centerbrook

A FTER ONE MEAL at Fine Bouche, you'll feel you've known chef-owner Steven Wilkinson forever. His personality pervades the lovely Victorian house he's made his restaurant, from the cartoons he posts in the outdoor display case to the mementos on the wall and, ultimately, to the meal on the plate. Wilkinson artfully straddles nouvelle and classic cuisine. Cognac spikes the lobster bisque, spiced pear garnishes the sautéed duck, and oyster mushrooms enhance wine-poached salmon. In all five courses of each prix-fixe dinner, the chef achieves a carefully honed balance of flavors. **(203) 767-1277. Lunch Tue–Fri 12–2. Dinner Tue–Sat 6–9, Sun 5–9. Closed Mon. Very expensive. MC, V.**

Old Lyme Inn

85 Lyme St, Old Lyme

AROUND southeastern Connecticut, the Old Lyme Inn is *the* place for dressy nights out. Tarted up with empire trappings and tapestried walls, the place is so quintessentially suburban preppie, you half expect to spot the ghost of John Cheever table-hopping. Observing patrons in evening dress and others tieless and Bean-booted, you may brace yourself for an evening of culinary schizophrenia. But pleasant surprises await you on your plate: hot oysters in a splendid champagne sauce, woodsy wild-mushroom soup, baby quail plumped with red currants. Our only cavil is with the overrich Chocolate Obsession. **(203) 434-2600. Lunch Tue–Sat 12–2. Dinner Tue–Sat 6–9, Sun from 12. Closed Mon. Reservations recommended. Very expensive. Cr.**

Restaurant du Village

59 Main St, Chester

RESTAURANT DU VILLAGE ought to be called Restaurant des Villages, considering the many provinces whose cuisines are represented on its eclectically Gallic menu.

The knowledgeable staff is quick to explain that calvados and caramelized apples on the *boudin blanc* indicate a Norman preparation, whereas the heady bouquet of lavender, orange peel, and other *herbes de Provence* accompanies dishes from southeast France. Our snouts-down favorites include the Périgord region's claim to culinary fame, truffles, which are employed here in many guises: in pâté, on pasta, atop roast chicken and duck. So committed is this restaurant to the cult of the mycophagists that it employs a globe-trotting collector to help stock the larder. **(203) 526-5301. Dinner Wed–Sun 5:30–9. Closed Mon–Tue. Reservations recommended. Very expensive. MC, V.**

....

T**HE GRISWOLD INN** (Main St, Essex) looks as if it's been through the war, and it has — the Revolutionary War; take a drink at the bar, but skip brunch, unless it's shad season . . . **The Gull Restaurant** (Pratt St, Essex) offers a fine view of the marina and a very good raw bar in the summer . . . Stop at **The Harbor View** (60 Water St, Stonington) for a snack in the lounge or dinner in the upscale back room . . . For a stellar brunch with a side of Bach, try **La Cuisine** (25 Whitfield St, Guilford), a storefront gourmet food shop with a superior bakery and café.

Litchfield County

Charles Bistro

51 Bank St, New Milford

IN A TOWN where second-rate burgers and third-rate pizza once reigned, suddenly there is the Charles Bistro, a charming French Provincial storefront with a real French chef. Although a few items, notably the bread, have not survived the ocean crossing, we are so pleased to see the greening of New Milford's culinary sward that we find it difficult to quibble. Oh, we could call the salmon bisque soft on flavor, but we prefer to remember its velvety texture and nuggets of fresh salmon. And surely, we have no complaint with the robust flavors of lightly sautéed veal and wild mushrooms. As for the luxuriant Grand Marnier–enhanced *crème brûlée:* perfection. **(203) 355-3266. Lunch Mon–Fri 11–3. Dinner Thur–Sat 6–9:30. Closed Sun. Expensive. N.**

Freshfields

Rte 128, West Cornwall

Wreshfields, perched HAT wonderfully affordable, non-neurotic New American dishes the young chef Steve Mangan turns out at Freshfields, perched over the Housatonic in an old-mill-stream setting. Wisely, since the location is perfect, the management concentrates on the food: chicken with jalapeño and *chèvre,* mako shark in pepper cream sauce, pasta with shrimps and scallops in Chardonnay sauce, impeccable vegetables, a knowing use of herbs. We couldn't be more pleased. **(203) 672-6601. Lunch Wed–Sat 12–2:30. Dinner Wed–Thur 5:30–9, Fri–Sat until 10, Sun 5–9. Sun brunch 11:30–2:30. Closed Mon–Tue. Reservations recommended. Expensive. MC, V.**

Holley Place

Pocketknife Sq, Lakeville

Dtifully restored nineteenth-century factory building, is enjoyable in the casual bar or the slightly more formal dining room. If you concentrate on the appetizers (like smoked trout and country pâté) and desserts (the Washington Depot ice cream may have no peer), you will fare well. But unfortunately, the more elaborate main courses are beyond this modest kitchen. If you must order an entrée, stay simple — as in calf's liver with onions. **(203) 435-2727. Dinner Wed–Thur 5:30–9, Fri–Sat until 10, Sun 4–8. Sun brunch 11:30–2. Closed Mon–Tue. Moderate. MC, V.**

The Pantry

Titus Rd, Washington Depot

IF YOU don't mind sitting among shelves of overpriced relishes and kitchen equipment, The Pantry is a delighful spot. It features marvelous soups like Green Garden, a puree of leeks and watercress, and tasty Ginger-Carrot. The rest of the menu is decidedly international, ranging from a boffo bouillabaisse teeming with shellfish to a Thai chicken curry. For dessert, there's trifle, and a chance to browse among coffee beans and wooden bunnies while you wait to pay the check. **(203) 868-0258. Beer and wine. Breakfast Tue–Sat 10–11:30. Lunch Tue–Sat 12–5:30, Sun 11–4. Closed Mon. Moderate. MC, V.**

Wickets

West St, Litchfield Commons, Litchfield

WICKETS calls itself a country eatery, when it's actually an au courant bistro of the most urbane sort. Attractive, even elegant, with a dusty rose color scheme and greenhouse dining area, it serves a brunch that goes pleasantly beyond the standard eggs Benedict. We found it strange, however, that an item described as "three kinds of smoked fish on spinach angel-hair pasta" arrived with one smoked fish and Canadian bacon on white spaghettini. Similarly, "poached eggs with hollandaise and white asparagus" arrived with carrots and snowpeas on wonderful potato-bacon pancakes. What you order here isn't what you get, but happily, all the surprises are pleasant. **(203) 567-8744. Lunch Tue–Sat 12:30–3. Dinner Tue–Wed 5:30–8, Thur until 9, Fri–Sat until 10. Sun brunch 12–4. Closed Mon. Moderate to expensive. Cr.**

....

The Yale Barn

Rte 44, East Canaan

BERKSHIRITES can thank invading New Yorkers not only for inflated real estate but for the presence of good ethnic dining. The Yale Barn, once the bastion of Boiled Bland, is now the province of a talented Taiwanese chef. Crowd favorites are the hot and spicy lamb and the Kung Po shrimp and scallops. Some guests may find remnants of the Occidental past disorienting (the Eric Sloane prints on the walls, blue cheese dressing on your salad), but there's no doubt about it: Chef Chen offers the best Chinese food for miles around. **(203) 824-5009. Lunch Tue–Sat 11:30–2. Dinner Tue–Thur 5–8, Fri–Sat until 9, Sun 11:30–8. Sun brunch until 3. Closed Mon. Moderate. AE, MC, V.**

....

OUTDOORS BY CANDLELIGHT? Visit **The Ragamont Inn** (Main St, Salisbury), which has a pleasant patio even if a rather traditional menu . . . **Fox & Fox** (Rte 7, Gaylordsville) has an inventive chef, a charming view of the Housatonic, and superior sweetbreads . . . There's nothing terribly tony about the **Mountain View Inn** (Rte 272, Norfolk), but the food is solid and one always leaves feeling like family.

Providence & Newport

Adesso

161 Cushing St, Providence

FROM THE MOMENT Adesso opened its doors, revealing the miraculous transfiguration of a bleak space in a garage-turned-shopping-mall into a sleek landscape of postmodern stainless and glass, it has been a magnet for all who glitter. The menu — California ethnic — includes a prosciutto with goat-cheese pizza that delights, and a delicious warm duck salad with radicchio and wild mushrooms. Cachet cuisine? Yup, and we love it. **(401) 521-0770. Sun–Thur 12–10:30, Fri–Sat until 11. No reservations. Expensive. AE, MC, V.**

Al Forno

7 Steeple St, Providence

WE KNOW a hedonist who occasionally drives three hours from his home in the Berkshires for a weekend in Providence. That way, he can dine two consecutive evenings at the wondrous Al Forno. His idea of dinner starts with an antipasto like none ever seen west of Verona, moves on to the exquisite Clams Al Forno, stops briefly at whatever pizza they're offering that night (calling one of these sublime creations "pizza," he says, is like calling a Latour '59 "grape juice"), settles for a while at one of the veal entrées, and concludes with a fruit tart ordered in advance. When he drives home Sunday he no longer fits in his car, but the smile on his face resembles the Mona Lisa's. **(401) 273-9760. Dinner Tue–Sat 5:30–10. Closed Sun–Mon. No reservations. Very expensive. AE, MC, V.**

....

Le Bistro

Bannister's Wharf, Newport

O F ALL THE good French restaurants we know, Le Bistro is the easiest to go back to, and not only because of the harbor view. Simplicity is the draw. Anise-scented bouillabaisse with a buttered baguette won't leave you dozing over the check; it's a fortifying lunch on a day you want to stick to afternoon plans. Nor is fresh blackfish in tart mustard sauce calculated to weigh heavy on the waistline. It's the kind of food you might fix for your family every day — if you were the *bonne femme* of a great French chef. **(401) 849-7778. Daily 11:30–11. Very expensive. Reservations recommended. Cr.**

....

The Black Pearl

Bannister's Wharf, Newport

Exuberant Sunday sailors wind-burned from a day on the waves find safe harbor at The Black Pearl. With its dark walls, window seats, low ceilings, and water views, this Newport institution is snug as an old wooden boat. The yacht club aesthetic extends to the menu, where pleasant surprises such as an herby clam chowder offset the regulation stuffed filet of sole and sherried seafood crêpes. **(401) 846-5264. Jackets. Lunch daily 11:30–1. Dinner 5:30–10. Reservations recommended. Expensive. Cr.**

Bluepoint Oyster Bar & Restaurant

99 North Main St, Providence

Neon lights and tall wooden booths, all vintage Sam Shepard, may help struggling artists from up the hill feel right at home, but they are poor stagings for the brilliant and beautiful food at the Bluepoint Oyster Bar & Restaurant. The mascot is treated with special tenderness here — fried, with sorrel mayonnaise on the side, this oyster is as bracing as a morning at sea. And if we were a monkfish, we'd demand an exclusive contract with the chef — cider beurre blanc is but one of the superb sauces she has devised to propel this ugly but talented fish from the cloister to stardom. **(401) 272-6145. Dinner Mon–Sun 6–11, Fri–Sat until 11:30. Very expensive. Cr.**

China Inn

285 Main St, Pawtucket

I F THERE WERE country clubs in Beijing, they would look like the new China Inn. Pale wood and upholstery in earth tones have replaced the fire-breathing-dragon decor of the old establishment, which was located next to a Laundromat on a remote Pawtucket side street. But even in that no-man's-land it bustled with happy diners every night of the week. Some say it's because of the flaming Pu-Pu platter and the hot-and-sour soup, thick with tree ears, shredded pork, and scallions. But we think it's the Peking duck, crisp *mooshi* pork, and peppery sweet scallops in Szechuan sauce that keep the devoted coming back for more. **(401) 723-3960. Sun–Thur 11:30 a.m.–11 p.m., Fri–Sat until midnight. Moderate. AE, MC, V.**

The Clarke Cooke House

Bannister's Wharf, Newport

A T The Clarke Cooke House, pheasant with wild rice and foie gras makes us as blissful (M.F.K. Fisher, forgive us) as fruit punch and brownies did when we were nine. A friend of ours swears that the sweetbreads in wine sauce here are the best he's had anywhere. No self-respecting Yankee would call this fashionably friendly restaurant, where the customers look as though they've just won at the roulette table, a bargain. But on the other hand, for those of us over the age of nine, how often does pleasure come this cheap? **(401) 849-2900. Jackets. Oct–May: Fri–Sat 6–10. June–Sept: daily 6–11. Reservations recommended. Very expensive. AE, MC, V.**

....

The Common's Lunch

The Common, Little Compton

H ONEST FOOD, based on local produce, happens to be in fashion everywhere right now, but it's never gone out of style at The Common's Lunch. A counter, some booths, and a view of the town green set off the culinary efforts: crisp, lacy johnnycakes, spicy quahog pie, and other Rhode Island specialties. Thick chowder and crunchy fritters are an especially appealing combination and make a hearty midday meal. Come early for lunch — everybody else in town does. **(401) 635-4388. Mon–Sat 6–6, Fri until 7 p.m., Sun 6–noon. Inexpensive. N.**

....

Estrela do Mar

736 North Broadway, East Providence

I T TAKES only a small leap to imagine yourself on a side street in Lisbon when you're dining at Estrela do Mar. At this festive restaurant, Portuguese is the local tongue and live *Fado* singing replaces the ubiquitous canned classical on weekend nights. The food here is not for the timid. After garlicky marinated quail and bowl of pungent *mariscada,* the clear, dry house white goes down like water. All that's missing is a postdinner stroll around the Rossio. **(401) 434-5130. Mon–Thur 11 a.m.–midnight, Fri–Sun 11:30–a.m.–1:30 a.m. Reservations recommended Fri–Sun. Moderate. AE, MC, V.**

....

Hemenway Sea Food

1 Old Stone Sq, Providence

Housed in the city's newest temple to lucre, Hemenway Sea Food has a million-dollar view of the Providence River and the lights of the city beyond. With so much money sunk in real estate, you might expect the management to cut corners on the food. But the grilled swordfish is moist and delicate, and the blackened Boston scrod is a delicious and — given the endangered status of redfish — thoughtful innovation. On Sunday evenings the huge dining room is often packed, so arrive early. **(401) 351-8570. Lunch Mon–Sat 11:30–3. Dinner Mon–Thur 5–10, Fri–Sat 4:30–11, Sun 11:30–10. Expensive. Cr.**

....

Leo's

99 Chestnut St, Providence

The clientele is a veritable Who's Who in Providence at this artists' mecca bustling with bluebloods and blue collars. Don't let the pub-style atmosphere distract you from the menu. Leo's serves a hot bowl of chili that's thick, meaty, and robust — a glorious concoction that cries for seconds. Look for the daily specials; nothing frozen here. Homemade desserts include mocha buttercrunch pie that'll crush the resolve of the most ardent dieter. **(401) 274-3541. Mon–Thur 11:30 a.m.–1 a.m., Fri until 2 a.m., Sat 5 p.m.–2 a.m., Sun 5 p.m.–1 a.m. Moderate. N, checks.**

Maharaja

303 South Main St, Providence

ANYONE WHO has eaten chicken *tikka* at Maharaja knows why India was the jewel in the crown. Pungent marinated meats and spiced breads, cooked in a barrel-shaped tandoor oven as you watch, are as far from the curries we used to call Indian as Peking duck is from chow mein. The Indian family that runs this place delights in educating guests to the pleasures of Punjabi cooking. Take a lesson. **(401) 421-5970. Dinner Tue–Sat 5:30–10, Sun 5–9:30. Closed Mon. Reservations recommended. Moderate. AE, MC, V.**

La Petite Auberge

19 Charles St, Newport

LA PETITE AUBERGE serves good French bar food at three-star prices. Decorated with lace tablecloths and antique furniture, it's a charming rendezvous for modern Madame Bovarys and their beloveds. Peppery fish soup, rich artichoke bottoms stuffed with ham and mushrooms, chicken with salsify in a dark sauce — all are good ways to start a heavy seduction scene. *Heavy* is the operative word here.

This robust peasant fare, adequate to fuel a Bordelaise grape grower at the height of the picking season, is delicious but leaves us groaning at the board. **(401) 849-6669. Dinner Mon–Sat 6–10, Sun 5–9. Reservations recommended. Jackets. Expensive. AE, CB, MC, V.**

....

P OT AU FEU owes its name to one of the glories of French cuisine, but such hearty dinner fare would be strictly déclassé in this sumptuously romantic salon, where the menu studiously recalls the Apician table of the Duchess of Guermantes. Such delicacies as oysters Florentine; veal with cream, brandy, and morels; and hazelnut and honey pie delight the refined palate even if the presentation (and the portions) are a little de trop. The crowded downstairs bistro is more low-key, offering uncomplicated supper food: savory crêpes stuffed with coq au vin, and pungent chicken with rosemary. On weeknights it's usually filled with hard-working overachievers too exhausted to whip up dinner at home. **(401) 273-8953. Lunch Mon–Fri 11:30–3. Dinner upstairs Tue–Thur 6–9, Fri–Sat until 10; jackets; reservations recommended. Dinner downstairs Sun 4–9, Mon–Thur 5–10, Fri–Sat until 11; no reservations. Expensive upstairs, moderate downstairs. Cr.**

....

Pot au Feu

44 Custom House St, Providence

Provender

3883 Main Rd, Tiverton

PROVENDER ARRIVED on this pastoral peninsula like an overdressed day-tripper from the big city. We shuddered whenever we drove through town as we pictured the expensive boutiques and fast cars that seemed guaranteed to follow. But even Thoreau tired of the simple life, we reminded ourselves as we stopped in one overcast, rainy afternoon, "just to look at the cheese." Soon we found ourselves at a little table by the window gobbling up turkey on thick slices of herb bread. The sandwich was called The Scarlet Letter, and by the time we'd dipped into a luscious spinach *roulade* and polished off a slice of cheesecake so creamy it almost cried moo, we'd been as pleasurably compromised as Hester Prynne. **(401) 624-9991. BYO. Daily 9–6. Moderate. AE, MC, V.**

Salas' Restaurant

345 Thames St, Newport

SALAS' RESTAURANT is one of the few places in downtown Newport where you can feed a family simply and well without mortgaging the farm. Lack of pretension is always an asset in this glitzy port, and although the management has opened a slick raw bar aimed at an upscale seasonal crowd, on the whole this Italian clam box lives up to its reputation. Chicken parmigiana and seafood salad, served in the downstairs dining room, are tasty and even commendable. You wouldn't spend your anniversary here, but it's a great place to let your three-year-old get entwined in spaghetti while you unwind with a beer. **(401) 846-8772. Upstairs dinner daily 4–10. Downstairs lunch May–Sept: Mon–Sat 11:30–3, Sun from noon; dinner daily 6–10. Raw bar (May–Sept) 11:30 a.m.–1 a.m. Moderate. AE, DC, MC, V.**

....

Wes'

1 Robar Plaza, Providence

EVEN THOSE OF US for whom barbecue is merely barbecue find Wes' an experience. A flaming pit the size of a swimming pool confronts you at the door. Masses of juicy ribs, charred lamb, and baby pig (Sundays only) sizzle above the grill in smoky magnificence. The ribs are a meaty handful, and the chicken manages to be delicately smoked on the outside, still juicy within. Beans, cornbread, and remarkably sweet cole slaw are the accompaniments of choice. **(401) 421-9090. Beer and wine. Mon–Thur 11:30 a.m.–2 a.m., Fri–Sat until 4 a.m., Sun 12–2 a.m. Inexpensive. N.**

....

White Horse Tavern

Marlborough and Farewell sts, Newport

AT THE White Horse, one of the oldest taverns in the country, waiters move through candlelight with the concentration of priests and the chef signs the menu. The food is old wine in nouvelle bottles — serious, pretty, and maddeningly uneven. We love the pungent ratatouille of five wild mushrooms and the lively tortellini with prosciutto, but wonder at the swordfish imprinted with a trendy grill grid but not the ginger marinade. Try an old standby, tender entrecote, instead. And bring money. **(401) 849-3600. Jackets. Lunch 12–3. Dinner 6–10. Sun brunch 12–3. Reservations required. Very expensive. Cr.**

....

FOR BEANSPROUTS and delicious homemade breads, there's **Amaras** (63 Warren Ave, East Providence) . . . **The Arboretum** (39 Warren Ave, East Providence) is for those special evenings when nothing less than gilding the lily will do . . . Recommended: the sauerkraut and sausages at **3 Steeple Street** (125 Canal St, Providence), right near RISD . . . The Pollo Cleopatra at the very Italian **Blue Grotto** (210 Atwells Ave, Providence) . . . And, finally, the sushi at **Tokyo Restaurant** (231 Wickenden St, Providence) has the style of fine jewelry and the price of a good fish fry.

Portland

OKAY, we'll admit it: we're biased. We have dined at Alberta's so well and so often that we have lost all critical distance. We don't even mind the Saturday night crush at the bar. The decor, compliments of local artists, changes almost as often as the adventuresome menu, a true masterpiece that on one evening included Oriental Shrimp-and-Chicken Eggroll, Hangtown Oyster Fry, sourdough eggplant pizza, and fettucine with scallops, lobster, peppers, and pine nuts. This is no mere nouvelle eatery, but a joint staffed with culinary genius. The food is fresh, the seasonings expert, and our devotion complete. **(207) 774-5408. Lunch Mon–Fri 11:30–2:30. Dinner Mon–Sat 5–10:30, Sun until 10. No reservations. Moderate to expensive. Cr.**

Alberta's

21 Pleasant St, Portland

The Baker's Table

434 Fore St, Portland

AFTER THE NEWER, glitzier Portland places have been considered and then dismissed, someone often says, "Let's go to The Baker's Table," and you're always glad you did. It serves the kind of food we'd make at home if we consistently had the time, incentive, and money. Totally undoctrinaire, the menu may give you a choice betweeen scallops baked with mushrooms in port and cognac, or garlicky baked haddock with tomatoes and herbs. There's always a distinguished bouillabaisse, classic tournedos, and desserts from the neighboring Port Bakehouse, which spawned the restaurant. The Bakehouse opens at 8 a.m. Sunday, and picking up fresh croissants or coffee cake along with the paper is a treasured routine for natives and highlanders alike. **(207) 775-0303. Lunch daily 11:30–2:30. Dinner Mon–Thur 5:30–9:30, Fri–Sat until 10, Sun until 9. Expensive. Cr.**

Café Always

47 Middle St, Portland

NOT FOR Café Always the muted mauves and grays, the discreet classical music, the single flower on the table that usually signals Serious Cuisine. *Au contraire,* baby, we're talkin' chrome-yellow oilcloth, black vinyl placemats, and wall art that looks like Louise Nevelson gone punk. But it is definitely serious about food. The proof? How about an appetizer of chicken medallions filled with veal and pork pâté in mustard cream sauce? For an entrée try roast pork tenderloin stuffed with apples, raisins, and pecans in reduced applejack sauce. Or the Thai chicken or the chicken-filled empanada. Which gives you some idea of the scope of the menu. **(207) 774-9399. Dinner Tue–Sun 5–10. Closed Mon. Moderate. AE, MC, V.**

F. Parker Reidy's

83 Exchange St, Portland

F. PARKER REIDY'S occupies a narrow and valuable slot in the Portland restaurant world — a really good place where the food is willing to defer to whatever business, social, or seduction scene you're into. You can count on your selection being fresh, well prepared, and cheerfully seasoned, but your meal doesn't constantly demand your attention. (Didja get that hint of fennel? How 'bout that silken texture!) The menu is strong on steaks and seafood, the service always friendly and usually competent, and the location right in the heart of the Yuppie Quarter. **(207) 773-4731. Mon–Sat 11:30 a.m.–12:30 a.m., Sun 4:30–11. Moderate. Cr.**

Gorham Station Restaurant

29 Elm St, Gorham

A FORMER Victorian-style railroad station, Gorham Station Restaurant has retained the authenticity and dignity of the original structure instead of lapsing into the kitschy-kitschy-cute that frequently overcomes restaurants with a theme. The food is in the same vein — simple and well done. Salad is serve yourself, and although the greens lack variety, they are accompanied by four very creditable dressings. Steaks, the mainstay of the menu, are cooked precisely to order. The dessert offering, mud pie, is a shameless attempt to pack as many calories as possible into a narrow wedge. **(207) 839-3354. Lunch Mon–Fri 11:30–2:30. Dinner Mon–Thur 5–10, Fri–Sat until 11, Sun 11:30–10. Moderate. AE, DC, MC, V.**

Hamilton's India Restaurant

43 Middle St, Portland

I F YOUR knowledge of authentic Indian food starts and ends with chicken curry, go ahead and put yourself in the capable hands of Hamilton's India Restaurant. Hamilton Ash, English-born owner of this downtown eatery, knows what he's doing, and his menu is helpful to initiates. It explains *raitas* as a "cooling counterpoint to spicy Indian dishes" and quick studies will find it's much more *pukka* to scoop up the food with *chapati* than to use a knife and fork. What we have here is hearty, intricately spiced cuisine that is prepared with obvious respect and served with a fine selection of beers. **(207) 773-4498. Dinner Sun, Tue–Thur 5:30–9, Fri–Sat until 10. Closed Mon. Moderate. AE, DC, MC, V.**

Maria's

337 Cumberland Ave, Portland

MARIA'S is an old-fashioned restaurant made for those occasions when you want to abandon your health maintenance diet in favor of cream, parmesan cheese, butter, and olive oil. The menu is traditional (Italian, of course), but the drama with which the waiter recites the specials of the day makes one feel downright revolutionary. Instead of anonymous house wines, you are offered a choice of something a little better (around twelve dollars a bottle) that's a fine accompaniment for shrimp sautéed with fresh tomatoes, black olives, and artichoke hearts. **(207) 772-9232. Mon–Thur 5–10, Fri–Sat until 11. Closed Sun. Expensive. MC, V.**

Moose Crossing

270 Rte 1, Falmouth

MOOSE CROSSING boldly disregards the anti-red meat movement, offering masterfully aged Iowa beef so tender that it actually can be cut with a fork. Surrounding that rare treat are accompaniments out of the ordinary: a house salad with shrimp and a peppery parmesan dressing, vegetables fresh and crisp enough to stand on their own, hot onion-rye and oatmeal rolls, and classic desserts that we liked better when we were sixteen. The difference between sirloin, tenderloin, and filet is explained with scholarly seriousness here. It's been some time since moose crossed where the restaurant stands, but it's still a convenient location. **(207) 781-4771. Mon–Thur 5–10, Fri–Sat until 11, Sun 4–10. Reservations recommended. Moderate. Cr.**

. . . .

Raoul's Roadside Attraction

865 Forest Ave, Portland

THE DECOR at Raoul's Roadside Attraction brings a deeper meaning to the word *eclectic*. A distinguished collection of hubcaps sets off the bar; the walls are adorned with peacock tails and pennants from Lisbon Falls High; the lighting is Early Roller Rink. Usually when a place looks like this the food tends to be mediocre. But notwithstanding the six-page, cartoon-scrawled menu, at Raoul's the food is good — not subtle, not light, but hearty and seasoned with a liberal hand. The hamburgers are thick, the Mexican Salad tests the old taste buds, and beers from twenty countries help put you in the spirit. If you're looking to join a clientele never found at the lobster houses, the sushi bars, or (God knows) the tea rooms, we highly recommend it. **(207) 775-2494. Mon–Sat 11:30 a.m.–1 a.m., Sun 1:30 p.m.–1 a.m. Inexpensive. MC, V.**

. . . .

Raphael's

36 Market St, Portland

RAPHAEL'S is the most ambitious restaurant to emerge in Portland in the past few years. The decor is formal mahogany, the cuisine Northern Italian, and the prices have a distinctly Boston flavor. They make a dead set at elegance, and generally succeed: valet parking, well-trained servers, matchbooks imprinted with your name — the kind of attention that makes a meal an occasion. The food mirrors the ambience: generally excellent with a few areas of overkill. The *gnocchi* in a tomato sauce sparked with Gorgonzola is zingy and delicate in texture, the veal dishes are of the highest quality, and the pasta is fresh and meltingly tender without softness. But a lone quail egg doesn't do much for a green salad, except justify the price. **(207) 773-4500. Lunch Mon–Fri 11:30–3. Dinner Sun–Thur 5–10, Fri–Sat until 11. Reservations recommended. Expensive. Cr.**

The Seaman's Club

375 Fore St, Portland

THE SEAMAN'S CLUB sits at the head of one of the prettiest streets in Portland, and if you're early enough to be seated by the arched windows, you can look down the cobblestoned way to the bustle of the waterfront. Though filet of sole with native crabmeat and seafood casserole may not win originality awards, they do remind you there's good reason for their popularity. In all, this restaurant presents New England cooking at its best, without seriously damaging your wallet. **(207) 772-7311. Lunch 11–2:30. Dinner 5:30–10. Sun brunch 10:30–3. Moderate. MC, V.**

West Side

58 Pine St, Portland

Y ou know you're in a neighborhood restaurant when every
head turns as you walk through
the door. The West Side is small with
minimal decor, as befits its local character, but the cook has definitely been to
Boston. The halibut with fresh ginger
and orange cream sauce is an excellent
blending of taste and texture, and the
fettucine with asparagus tips and artichoke hearts is both light and rich, no
easy trick. Besides the four or five dinner
entrées, which change weekly, there are
selected appetizers and light dinners, and
a seafood-stuffed phyllo that makes you
glad you're in the neighborhood. **(207)
773-8223. Breakfast Mon–Sat 7–11. Lunch
Mon–Sat 11:30–2:30. Dinner daily 5:30–10.
Sun brunch 9–2:30. Moderate. AE, MC, V.**

The Whistling Oyster

Perkins Cove, Ogunquit

F orty-five minutes is too long to
wait for an appetizer, especially
when the lovely antique chairs are
breaking your spine. This said, praise
for The Whistling Oyster can proceed.
Here, even a bottle of Orvieto gets the
full wine routine, and once dinner gets
under way, dishes appear and disappear
with nicely underplayed dexterity. We
suggest a small selection of smoked fish,
sauced with horseradish and cream as an
appetizer and, for the main course, homemade fettucine with tomato and fresh
basil. The vegetables with this entrée,

by the way, are five Chinese pea pods and two cauliflowerets, which may be carrying understatement a bit too far. **(207) 646-9521. Lunch Mon–Sat 12–2:30. Dinner Mon–Fri 6–9:30, Sat until 10. Closed Sun. Reservations recommended. Expensive. Cr.**

....

Wormwood's

Bay Ave, Camp Ellis Beach, Saco

WORMWOOD'S is a barn of a restaurant tucked among tiny camps on the edge of spectacular ocean scenery. Relaxing, down-home friendliness mingles with a healthy respect for seafood. Lobster, clams, and shrimp are cooked to order without any attempt to "improve" on flavor. When the chef does get fancy, it generally doesn't work, as in the alarmingly orange crumb topping smothering sweet and tender meat in the crab pie. Use common sense when ordering and you'll have a delightful meal, and the atmosphere will make you feel better about the human race. **(207) 282-9679. Daily 11:30–10, Sun until 9. Moderate. MC, V.**

....

B OTH THE best breakfast in Portland and the most casual atmosphere are to be found at the **Good Egg Cafe** (705 Congress St, Portland) . . . **Hu Shang III** (33 Exchange St, Portland) has lost its original luster, but nothing has come to fill the void; if you feel like Chinese, it's still the place in town . . . The regional Italian cooking at **Luna D'Oro** (41 Middle St, Portland) is as good or better than Raphael's, with lower prices and a cozier atmosphere . . . **The Gallery** (215 Foreside Rd, Falmouth Foreside) offers the most dramatic boat-and-bay views around — just don't plan on being thrilled by the food . . . If you want to experience the ornate "cottages" that housed the summer rich of yesteryear, choose **Camp Hammond** (74 Main St, Yarmouth); the cooking is almost as impressive as the building . . . **Madd Apple Café** (23 Forest Ave, Portland) has survived a change of ownership and continues to serve idiosyncratic meals at reasonable prices.

Maine Coast

O N A SLOW NIGHT you may catch David Grant, chef-owner of Camden's Aubergine, trading gourmet secrets with patrons at the inn's elegant parlor-style bar. Trained in France, he speaks the language with grand affectation. But a few bites into dinner and you'll have to concede that he's earned his glottal *R*s, along with a couple of stars. Diners who take the "do me" route, a four-course prix-fixe meal with appropriate wines by the glass, might start off with creamy leek flan flanked by Belon oysters and American caviar or ravioli of smoked trout with truffle butter. Every subsequent dish measures up, right through a raspberry tart for dessert. **(207) 236-8053. Open spring–fall only, Tue–Sun 6:30–9. Closed Mon. Reservations required. Very expensive. Cr.**

Aubergine

6 Belmont Ave, Camden

Brightside Restaurant

15 Main St, Belfast

FINDING A GOOD PLACE for breakfast in a small town when you're on the road is a treat, which is why you should know about the Brightside. Breakfast here could be a thick slice of apricot bread beside translucent slices of kiwifruit and a spoonful of apricot preserves. This, plus great coffee and two broiled slices of bacon, and you may be tempted to return for lunch. Any time of day, the whole place shines with enthusiasm. **(207) 338-4779. Beer and wine. Mon–Fri 7 a.m.–2 p.m., Sat–Sun 8–1. Inexpensive. N.**

··

Dolphin Marina

Basin Point Rd (off Rte 123), South Harpswell

ANYONE who has lived in Maine long enough has a favorite place down by the shore. Ours is at the end of a fifteen-mile dead end and well worth the journey. The Dolphin Marina is really two restaurants in one: the men who work the waters around South Harpswell eat cheeseburgers at the counter, and the blue-rinse set from Brunswick occupies the tables overlooking Casco Bay, blissing out on the view, the home-baked muffins, and the fresh, seasonal fruit pies. The lobster stew, packed with chunks of meat, drenched with cream and butter, may be equaled at greater price elsewhere but not surpassed. **(207) 833-6000. Daily 8–8. Inexpensive to moderate. MC, V.**

··

Estes Lobster House

Rte 123, South Harpswell

ESTES LOBSTER HOUSE is the heart and soul of summer in Maine. It's fifteen miles from the closest town on an isthmus near a tiny summer-cottage and fishing village, so the tourists are largely Mainers wandering around their own state taking all that beauty and pure air for granted. The lobster boat outside the window plays the Grateful Dead at concert strength, and the long box of a building usually swarms with somewhat gritty children. The food is simple: boiled lobster, steamed clams, and a haddock sandwich that can't be beat, since the fish has so lately leapt out of the ocean. If calling food "honest" didn't sound so condescending, that's what we'd do. **(207) 833-6340. Open Memorial Day–Labor Day. Beer and wine. Daily 11:30–9. Inexpensive. N.**

Firepond's

Main St, Blue Hill

FIREPOND'S SETTING is so charming, a clapboard house nestled streamside in a granite-walled ravine, that the cuisine could be less than consummate and no one would complain. All the more credit is due, then, for presentations as delicious as they are pretty: an elegant galantine of pheasant, for instance, and a thick slice of Atlantic salmon expertly steamed *en papillote*. Despite the circulating bread tray and a substantial wedge of hazelnut praline cheesecake, you'll come away feeling

well nourished rather than force-fed.
(207) 374-2135. Dinner 5–9:30. Reservations recommended. Expensive. AE, DC, MC, V.

....

Le Garage

Water St, Wiscasset

L E GARAGE, as the name implies, is in a redone garage just off Wiscasset's main street. Tables set out on a long, airy porch overlook the Sheepscot River. Despite the macho name, the cuisine is designed to please the Ladies' Trade. It has the strengths of this type of cooking: fresh ingredients, attractive presentation, an imaginative use of herbs. It also has the drawbacks: nothing you bite will bite back, either in texture or in seasoning. There are lots of crêpes and omelettes, and desserts tend toward custards and bread pudding. Order a glass of white wine, however, and it comes in a goblet suitable for breeding goldfish, which may be why Aunt Mildred recommends the place so highly. **(207) 882-5409. Lunch Mon–Sat 11:30–2:30. Dinner Mon–Sat 5–9, Sun from noon. Reservations recommended. Moderate. CB, DC, MC, V.**

....

The Haven

Main St (at the town dock), Vinalhaven

L IKE MANY an unspoiled Down East island, Vinalhaven tends to favor inconspicuous consumption. So you'd never suspect that behind The Haven's ordinary storefront there lurks a restaurant every bit as recherché as the coastal competition—California's coast, that is. Consider the julienne of jicama and smoked chicken lavished with raspberry vinaigrette, or the crab-stuffed sole, a paean to the largesse of the sea. We think these folks are hiding their light under a bushel. **(207) 863-4969. BYO. Breakfast Tue–Sat 5:30–11, Sun 7–11. Lunch Tue–Fri 11:30–1:30. Dinner Tue–Sat at 6 and 8, by reservation. Call for schedule off-season. Moderate. N, checks.**

....

Kristina's
160 Center St, Bath

KRISTINA'S started life as a bakery, developed a fringe of tables around the display cases, and now serves full meals as well as a super Sunday brunch. It's still a local place, catering largely to Bath residents, but it's worth the brief detour off Route 1 on your way up the coast. Vegetables Alfredo is a suave yet assertive blend of textures and flavors, and there's a three-layer puff-pastry sandwich—filled with seafood salad, avocado, and bacon— that we haven't seen anywhere else. Go there prepared to have dessert, perhaps the Orange Walnut Pie or the French Mint Cheesecake. The high-quality ingredients and wholesome atmosphere will surely counteract the calories. **(207) 442-8577. Sun 9 a.m.–11 p.m., Mon 7 a.m.–2 p.m., Tue–Sat 7 a.m.–9 p.m. Moderate. N.**

....

Maurice
Restaurant
Français

113 Main St, South Paris

WHEN YOU find a decent restaurant in an unlikely location, there's a tendency to overpraise it. Okay, so Maurice Restaurant Français is not a flawless gem tucked away within earshot of the Oxford Speedway. It does offer old-fashioned French food cooked with care and served in a handsome former private home. The pleasant staff is acquainted with such niceties as finger bowls and the difference between a white-wine glass and a red-wine glass. But a maraschino cherry on top of duck à l'orange, however crisp the skin, is tacky. The pâté du chef is rough and deeply flavored; the bread fresh, hot, and crusty; and the peach crisp with heavy cream reason enough to make the hour-plus drive from Portland. **(207) 743-2532. Lunch Mon–Fri 11:30–1:30. Dinner Sun–Thur 5–9, Fri–Sat until 9:30. Sun brunch 11–2. Reservations recommended. Moderate. Cr.**

Mill Race

Main St, Vinalhaven

ROUGH AND ROOMY as a Grange hall, the Mill Race gives you Maine instead of nautical knickknacks. The tables sport red oilcloths and bouquets in barnacled Coke bottles. Your blueberry muffin comes straight from the oven, with a slab of butter and a mason jar of jelly. For a change, you might order eggs with fishcakes, not ones that resemble lumps of library paste, but peppery, potato–packed patties that taste like solid chowder. Add a view of a quiet cove and some country licks on the radio, and you're talking road-food hall of fame. **(207) 863-9366. BYO. Breakfast 5–11:30. Lunch 11:30–2. Dinner Fri–Mon 6–9. Moderate. N, traveler's checks.**

....

The Red Barn

Main St (Rte 1), Milbridge

T HE RED BARN, forty miles up the coast from Bar Harbor, in Milbridge, is a place where the boys in rubber boots pour their own coffee in the morning and talk lobster prices. Try the crab stew at lunch and any of the seafood at night. Portions are for serious eaters: the Mate's Platter can feed nine or so, and even the so-called Mini-mate has proved too much for a friend who's a former shot-putter. The pancakes *should* have more blueberries, though, seeing how many millions of pounds are produced here each year. **(207) 546-7721. Mon–Sun 7 a.m.–9 p.m., Sun 8 a.m.–9 p.m. Reservations recommended. Moderate. N.**

....

Rock Ovens

Rte 24, Bailey Island

Y OU'D THINK a spectacular drive, a location almost completely surrounded by ocean, islands, and fishing boats, and the freshest of fish, scallops, and lobster would be enough for a restaurant. Rock Ovens adds to components missing from most other lobster houses: a pleasant, non-plastic decor and attention to detail that make the entire meal a pleasure. Admittedly, it's difficult to ruin a boiled lobster, but the bag of soggy potato chips that frequently accompanies it, along with the processed cole slaw, can benefit from upgrading. Here you'll find warm whole wheat rolls, an excellent side dish of red cabbage and apples, and even a decent salad. It's a professional duty to order the killer dessert at any restaurant, and the orange cheesecake with chocolate glaze made our sacrifice worthwhile. **(207) 833-6911. Dinner Wed–Mon 5–9. Closed Tue. Reservations required. Moderate. MC, V.**

Sail Loft

Rockport Harbor, Rockport

THE SAIL LOFT is a classic, and like so many classics it combines genuine quality with a tendency to put you to sleep. The lobster stew cannot be improved: crowded with chunks of tail and claw, rich with cream and butter, it has the sweet scent of the sea throughout. From there on, however, both menu and preparation lapse into apathy. Baked stuffed shrimp, broiled chopped beefsteak, and sole with lemon and capers have to be very, very good to transcend their lack of originality. But the restaurant's location at the Rockport Marina, on the edge of a prototypical little harbor, does make up for a lot. **(207) 236-2330. Lunch Mon–Sat 11:30–2:30, Sun 12–2:30. Dinner daily 5:30–8:30. Reservations recommended. Moderate. Traveler's checks.**

....

C HANGING ITS MENU daily, 22 Lincoln allows the chef to be as inventive as he likes. Guests can sample the fruits of his labor via a "Menu Dégustation," a dinner of six minicourses that hits all the highlights. A salad selection of thinly sliced smoked duck breast and slivered endive with a suave walnut oil dressing is a bold and successful play of textures and flavors. Other choices, such as the ragout of lobster and sweetbreads and the flounder with oysters and chives, reflect the chef's youthful approach to cooking. The service? On one visit, a waiter tripped on a doorsill, staggered, and flailed his way to our table. "That was the entertainment," he said, regaining his balance. "Now, may I take your order?" That's style. **(207) 725-5893. Sun, Tue–Thur 6:30–9, Fri–Sat 6–9:30. Lounge open until 11:30 p.m. Closed Mon. Reservations recommended. Expensive. AE, MC, V.**

22 Lincoln

22 Lincoln St, Brunswick

....

DINING OUT on the Maine Coast is a strictly seasonal affair, so unless otherwise noted, the following are open only from Memorial Day ,through Columbus Day . . . **Oak Point** (in tiny Trenton) offers a classic lobster-pound experience, as well as views of Mount Desert Island and Cadillac Mountain . . . Speaking of classics, you can't ignore **Jordan Pond House** on the loop road in Acadia National Park; even though the old building burned, they still offer tea and those great popovers in a spectacular setting . . . **The Waterfront Restaurant,** as one might suspect, is perched right on Camden harbor; you can get fried clams here, but they also have shrimp with feta and smoked chicken salad, all for reasonable prices (open all year) . . . California hasn't gained a toehold at **Le Domaine** (Rte 1, Hancock), which has the feeling and the superb cooking of a French country inn . . . **The Manor** (Battle Ave, Castine) is a restored summer cottage now serving as an inn; seafood is the specialty here — but expect Belon oysters in periwinkle-and-caviar sauce rather than lobster roll.

Southern
New Hampshire

Y OU CAN trace the lineage of the Bedford Village Inn and Restaurant by the cows grazing in surrounding pastures, the wide pine boards of the several dining rooms, dill picked fresh from the garden, and sausage made in the inn's kitchen. The house, which dates from 1810, is a mix of period paintings, oriental rugs, and original wood paneling, and the food is its equal in elegance. Crabmeat-stuffed artichoke hearts and lobster fettucine followed by a roasted duck in orange sauce are served in what once must have been the master bedroom. Rich surroundings and an eye for detail make the familiar exquisite. **(603) 472-2001. Lunch Mon–Sat 11:30–2. Dinner Mon–Wed 5:30– 9:30, Thur–Sat until 10, Sun 3–9. Sun brunch 11–2. Expensive. AE, DC, MC, V.**

Bedford Village Inn and Restaurant

2 Old Bedford Rd, Bedford

The Birchwood Inn

Rte 45, Temple

THE BIRCHWOOD INN is the quintessential New England hostelry, a family-operated, lovingly restored original nestled along a quiet town common. There's a limited menu that changes daily, and owner-chef Bill Wolfe continually transforms simple meat and fish dishes into a series of pleasant surprises. There isn't a hint of phoniness here, from the food to the original eighteenth-century murals in the small, candlelit dining room. **(603) 878-3285. BYO. Dinner Tue–Sat 6–9. Closed Sun–Mon. Reservations required. Moderate. N, checks.**

Blue Strawbery Restaurant

29 Ceres St, Portsmouth

WILD STRAWBERRY FIELDS once flourished on the site of the Blue Strawbery Restaurant, but that isn't what makes it so admirable. Nor is it the waiters, so strikingly handsome that we often feel we're dining in a menswear ad, so highfalutin in their speech that we've been asked — cross our hearts — "Have you had a sufficiency?" No, what makes the Strawbery one of the best, most innovative restaurants in New England is its talented chef, James Haller, a man who relishes taking risks in the kitchen — be it stuffing trout with lobster mousse, or quail with walnut cheese and smoked mussels. He's even, gulp, served sweetbreads in a chocolate brandy sauce. The dining room is intimate brick, the china eclectic Wedgewood, the only dessert, strawberries of course, served with brown sugar and sour cream. **(603) 431-6420. Dinner seatings May–mid-Oct: Mon–Sat at 6 and 9, Sun at 3 and 6; winter: Tue–Thur at 7:30, Fri–Sat at 6 and 9, Sun at 3 and 6. Closed Mon off-season. Reservations required. Very expensive. N.**

....

Cafe Guerriero

222 West St, Keene

AFE GUERRIERO has just enough of a classy edge to whet the appetites of locals looking for an upscale evening. Although meat, potatoes, and even the all-American hamburger are now on the menu, the original Northern Italian cuisine is where the chef continues to shine. The pasta is fresh and imaginative; we took ours as chicken tortellini and broccoli served in a butter-and-garlic sauce. Order the veal, but leave room for lemon mousse. **(603) 357-4353. Mon–Sat 11:30–10, Sun until 8:30. Expensive. Cr.**

....

La Cantina

Rte 114 and Donald St, Bedford

A CANTINA is as gritty as a cowboy hangout on the outskirts of Fort Worth. It's dark and a little seedy around the edges, but the food is plentiful, spicy, and reassuring. Couple a platter of enchiladas or burritos with a bottomless basket of nacho chips and a super-sized margarita, and you'll feel like a gringo gone native. **(603) 624–8757. Lunch Mon–Fri 11:30–2. Dinner Mon–Wed 5–9, Thur until 10, Fri–Sat until 11. Closed Sun. Moderate. Cr.**

....

Chalkboard West

222 West St, Keene

C HALKBOARD WEST is just the kind of restaurant that fits in with Keene's sudden boom — a friendly, unpretentious place in the seminal Colony Mill Marketplace. You can almost hear the thrum of the heavy machinery that was moved out just a few years ago (maybe that's why a nervous waitress spilled a carafe of wine in our lap). Still, our meals here have been enjoyably understated. Black Angus beef is a specialty, and they actually know how to broil sea scallops without turning them to rubber. **(603) 357–1909. Lunch Mon–Sat 11:30–5. Dinner Mon–Sat 5–10, Sun 11:30–7. Reservations recommended. Expensive. Cr.**

....

Codfish Aristocracy

The Hill, Portsmouth

T HE MENU of Portsmouth's Codfish Aristocracy — The Codfish, to locals — is a catalog of all the food trends that have journeyed down the pike in the past ten years. But trendy or not, this is good stuff when done honestly and inexpensively, and The Codfish passes muster. A superb pizza (need we add, tomato *or* pesto?) can be topped with garlic, shrimp, and black olives in addition to the usual laminations. **(603) 431-8503. Daily 11:30–11. Entertainment (light rock) downstairs nightly. Moderate. AE, MC, V.**

....

The Folkway
85 Grove St, Peterborough

A FTER A DECADE of settling comfortably into its countercultural style, The Folkway has avoided the rampant trendification that's swallowing the rest of Peterborough. The kitchen serves up a deliciously eclectic, always-made-from-scratch menu, with such standbys as fragrant chicken rosemary always available. The veal, pasta, and fish dishes are daily-changing adventures, and Mexican Night comes every Thursday. **(603) 924-7484. Tue–Sat 11 a.m.–10:30 p.m. Sun brunch 11–2. Closed Mon. Reservations recommended. Moderate. MC, V.**

....

The Grill and the True Blue Cafe
6 Ceres St, Portsmouth

I F THE NAME of the game among Portsmouth restaurants is to see who can get closest to the tugboats, The True Blue Cafe has won. Any closer and you'd need to show a union card. But this place scores well in other respects, too. The appetizers are elegant; baked Brie with walnuts and apple slices is a beguiling kickoff. As for entrées, the peppery linguine with squid strikes a precise balance between delicate and pungent. Add fresh-squeezed juices, fruity daiquiris, an uncommonly pleasant fleet of waitresses, and who cares about a bunch of silly tugboats? **(603) 431–6700. Daily 11:30–11. Moderate. CB, DC, MC, V.**

....

The Grill at Portsmouth Harbor

Bow and Ceres sts, Portsmouth

COMMANDING a harbor view at the head of Ceres Street, The Grill at Portsmouth Harbor juggles exposed beams, pink decor, and eighties minimalism. On the menu, yet more felicitous contrasts: smoked eel with dilled cream cheese, cod cheeks and monkfish tails in herbed tomato broth, sole sauced with sherry and black beans. The combinations work — they're imaginative but never wacky. The individual rack of lamb is a more straightforward note, served rare, as it must be. The homage to red peppers is almost trendy, but they're agreeable enough and, like all vegetables here, treated with respect. **(603) 431–6700. Lunch Mon–Sat 11:30–3:30. Dinner daily 5–10. Sun brunch 11:30–3:30. Reservations recommended. Expensive. DC, MC, V.**

....

Karen's

105 Daniel St, Portsmouth

WHEN WE'RE IN Portsmouth and we don't want to get dressed up, when we're not in the mood (or purse) for places named Strawbery, when we want to warm our souls and toes in front of a chilly-day fire, and especially when we're looking for breakfast, we head for Karen's. We particularly applaud the homemade bread, cardamom coffee cake, russet-skinned home fries, fresh fruit garnishes, and *real* corned-beef hash. **(603) 431-1948. BYO. Breakfast Mon–Sat 7–11:30. Lunch Mon–Sat 11:45–3. Dinner Tue–Thur 5–9, Fri–Sat until 10. Sun brunch 8–2. Inexpensive to moderate. N.**

....

Millstone

1 Eagle Sq, Concord

SURROUNDED BY legions of ferns and muted earth tones, you might expect Millstone to be yet another flashy joint that uses ambience to hide mediocre food. But how wrong you'd be. From a spicy appetizer of seafood sausage to a rich brownie sundae, this place pays attention to both taste and presentation. The chef shines at preparing duck — with a honey, Dijon mustard, and sesame seed glaze. Go for lunch and you can rub elbows with state politicos. **(603) 228-1982. Lunch Mon–Sat 11:30–2:30. Dinner Mon–Sat 5:30–9, Sun 11–7. Reservations recommended. Expensive. AE, MC, V.**

....

Pond View

Rte 125, Kingston

THE POND VIEW is a throwback to the great days of Beef. There's a big, traditional menu with plenty of steak and seafood, but you should opt for the prime rib. The Liberal cut (Conservative is smaller) consists of two ribs — you don't cut it, you quarry it. But for all the emphasis on portion size, quality isn't neglected. The beef is tender and flavorful (although accompanying vegetables are sometimes lackluster), the ambience is Sunday-dinner American, and the window tables do present the promised view. **(603) 642-5556. Lunch Mon–Sat 11:30–3. Dinner Mon–Fri 3–9, Sat until 10, Sun 12–9. Sun brunch until 3. Expensive. N.**

Powder Mill Pond Restaurant

Rte 202, Bennington

THE Powder Mill Pond Restaurant doesn't attempt to disguise itself as yet another "authentic" New England inn. Its white walls and simple furnishings won't draw your attention from the carefully prepared food. After fifteen years cooking for major hotels, owner-chef Jerry Willis opened the restaurant in what was once his grandmother's farmhouse, and his fastidious concern for taste and presentation is obvious. Willis's menu leans toward meat and potatoes; English Beefsteak heaped with paper-thin onion rings and succulent Mountain Chicken with sage stuffing are prime examples. **(603) 588-2127. Lunch Tue–Fri 11:30–2. Dinner Tue–Sat 5–9, Sun 11–3. Closed Mon. Reservations recommended. Moderate. MC, V.**

Szechuan Taste

54 Daniel St, Portsmouth

WHEN IT OPENED in Portsmouth a few years ago, Szechuan Taste ended the Serious Chinese Food Vacuum north of Boston's suburbs. We drop in often to make sure entropy hasn't set in, and so far we're happy. The kitchen is still doing most things right. Flavors remain subtle yet separate, portions generous. Recommended: the crispy whole fish, a crackly, split cod topped with a fruity sauce of onions and sweet peppers. **(603) 431-2226. Sun–Thur 11:30–10, Fri–Sat until 11. Moderate. Cr.**

THE **John Hancock Inn** (Main St, Hancock) is the state's oldest continuously operating inn; the fare's only fair, but the surroundings can't be duplicated . . . **Sa-La Thai** (Rte 63, Amherst) brings Thai food to New Hampshire . . . If you can overlook the minuscule portions and the sky-high prices, you'll find cutting-edge cuisine at the **Boilerhouse** (Rte 202, South Peterborough) . . . For continental breakfasts and fine French pastry, **Ceres Bakery** (51 Penhallow St, Portsmouth).

White Mountains

Bernerhof Inn

Rte 302, Glen

WITH ALL THE hype and hoopla, it's easy to overlook the fact that eating is essentially a very simple pleasure. The next time you need reminding, head to the Bernerhof Inn, which, despite its shrine status, serves basic Swiss bourgeois fare: veal stew, for instance, on a bed of plump parsleyed spaetzle, or profiterole *au chocolat,* the grown-up's hot-fudge sundae. Only the *délice de Gruyère* (a house specialty resembling breaded fondue bars) lacks the requisite luster. Look for it, instead, in a scintillating glass of Steinhäuser beer. This is the kind of meal you long for after a day on the slopes. **(603) 383-4414. Lunch (summer and fall) 12–3. Dinner 6–9:30. Sun brunch 11–2:30. Closed Easter–Memorial Day, mid-Nov to mid-Dec. Expensive. AE, MC, V.**

EAGLE MOUNTAIN HOUSE, overlooking Jackson, is another local grand hotel that got the phoenix treatment. The restoration works, right down to the rockers on the wraparound porch, the gramophone that graces the lobby, and the dining room's chicken pot pie topped with a superlative, classic crust. Each dish delights, from mushroom caps stuffed with sausage and almonds to a trufflelike chocolate cheesecake. The house wine could use an upgrade (Dourthé really ought to be relegated to the pantry), but in every other respect the Eagle flies right. **(603) 383-9111. Breakfast 7–9. Lunch 11:30–1:30. Dinner 6–9. Sun brunch 11:30–2. Reservations recommended. Expensive. AE, MC, V.**

Eagle Mountain House

Carter Notch Rd, Jackson

REMINISCENT OF college-town eateries, Hooligans seems to emphasize simple favorites and large portions. The potato skins have enough potato left on them to pass for home fries, and an order for one — piled high and flooded with melted cheese — is enough for four. Entrées and desserts are equally voluminous, stacks of ribs barbecued in a spicy sauce and wedges of mud pie too large to finish. Service is great and can even include an update on the ball game on TV in the bar. **(603) 356-6110. Daily 11–11. Moderate. AE, MC, V.**

Hooligans

Kearsarge St, North Conway

The Inn at Thorn Hill

Thorn Hill Rd, Jackson Village

OUR SEARCH for an ideal country getaway in the White Mountains ended with The Inn at Thorn Hill. Not only is it stylish as all get-out (the work of a youngish Stanford White), but the food comes in pleasantly adequate portions with just enough nouvelle flair. Sometimes art surpasses substance, as in a pretty puree of winter squash that disappoints in the tasting. But you'll find such missteps insignificant in the face of hand-formed crabmeat ravioli garnished with plump oyster mushrooms, or the divine chocolate-doused pear tartlet. This is one place we'd stay anytime: pastures just don't get any greener. **(603) 383-4242. Dinner 6–9:30. Reservations recommended. Very expensive. AE, MC, V.**

J. E. Henry's Restaurant and Tavern at the Mill

Kancamagus Hwy, Lincoln

IF William "The Refrigerator" Perry were to dine at Loon Mountain's Tavern at the Mill, he wouldn't be disappointed. Portions are gargantuan: the open-faced steak sandwich is sufficient to serve the entire Chicago Bears defensive line (or the compact equivalent, one hungry thirteen-year-old). The menu ranges from burgers to seafood, and the food is good, provided you keep it simple. **(603) 745-3603. Breakfast daily 7–11. Lunch 11:30–3. Dinner Mon–Thur 5–9, Sat–Sun until 10:30. Moderate. Cr.**

Sally's

Rte 302, Bartlett Center

BARTLETT is the town that development forgot (so far), and Sally's is the tin-ceilinged dining room of the newly refurbished but old-fashioned Bartlett Hotel. The breakfasts here are fit for lumberjacks, complete with a fine corned-beef hash. Sally hasn't been sighted yet, but Vinny, the new proprietor, hails (we hear) from New York City and Provincetown, which explains the artwork hung three tiers high on the pink walls. **(603) 374-6151. Wed–Sun 7 a.m.–9 p.m. Call for hours during spring. Moderate. N.**

Stonehurst Manor

Rte 16, North Conway

ONCE HOME to the Bigelow family, Stonehurst Manor fulfills every fantasy of life in the Gilded Age. Surrounded by dark oak and stained glass, diners are ushered by tuxedoed waiters to tables elaborate with crystal and fine linen, where they wait — and wait — for exquisitely memorable meals. Pork tenderloin is bathed in sauce of Marsala, walnuts, and peppers. Filet mignon cuts like butter. But be prepared: on our last visit, we arrived for dinner at nine, and it was eleven before we received our main course. The lines are probably shorter pre- or post-ski season. **(603) 356-3113. Dinner daily 6–10. Reservations required. Very expensive. AE, MC, V.**

Wildcat Inn and Tavern

Rte 16A, Jackson

Before you start a day of intensive cross-country skiing, may we suggest a bowl of *birchesmüsli* at the Wildcat Inn and Tavern just across the road from the Jackson Ski Touring Center. This popular Swiss concoction blends oatmeal with various fresh and dried fruits, and is tossed with generous gobs of thick whipped cream. Throw in a few apple pancakes with salty slabs of smokehouse ham, a warm-from-the-oven wedge of blackberry coffee cake, and you're fuel-injected for forty below. **(603) 383-4245. Breakfast 7:30–9:30. Lunch 11:30–3. Dinner Sun–Thur 6–9, Fri–Sat until 10. Moderate to expensive. AE, MC, V.**

If you're passing through Frost country during the warmer months, stop at **Polly's Pancake Parlor** (Rte 117, Sugar Hill) — a postcard-pretty carriage shed where several generations of sapaholics have been making flapjacks for close to fifty years . . . **Yesterdays** (Jackson Village) is really just a lunch (and breakfast) room, but the Monte Cristo is overstuffed and the brownie sundaes state-of-the-art . . . Scottish food may, frankly, rate right down there with English, but consider shortbread, trifle, and the mysteries of bubble-and-squeak at **The Scottish Lion** (Rte 16, North Conway) . . . For dining in the romantic Victorian mode, there's the *très chic* and *très cher* **Plum Room** at the Wentworth Resort Hotel (Jackson Village).

Upper Valley

A T THE Barnard Inn, arguably the best restaurant in Vermont, the old beamed-ceiling dining rooms glow with fire and candlelight. Its country location, ten miles north of Woodstock, requires a pleasant detour. The changing seasons bring wild mushrooms, fiddlehead ferns, and, for the roast duck, delighful sauces of fresh elderberry, plum, or frost grape. Even the lowly broccoli stem is elevated: pared and steamed to sweet tenderness, it gives one a whole new respect for a part of the plant they used to throw away. **(802) 234-9961. Jackets. June–Sept: Sun, Tue–Thur 6–9; Fri–Sat until 9:30; closed Mon. Oct–May: closed Mon–Tue. Reservations recommended. Very expensive. AE, MC, V, checks.**

Barnard Inn

Rte 12, Barnard, Vt.

Café la Fraise

**8 West Wheelock St,
Hanover, N.H.**

FROM THE blueberry soup to the raspberry mousse, the menu at Café la Fraise is fruity and feminine. Two talented local ladies have created an elegant, comforting place for a candlelight dinner or an upscale lunch. In the kitchen, delicate, almost frothy foods are conjured (a smoked salmon mousse with dill sauce, shrimp in brandy and cream). In the two small dining rooms, the wallpaper and table linens subtly reflect the berry motif. But the stouthearted need not feel bereft: there's a seven-ounce filet on the menu, too. **(603) 643-8588. Lunch Tue–Sat 11:30–2. Dinner Tue–Thur 6–9, Fri–Sat until 9:30. Reservations recommended. Expensive. MC, V.**

D'Artagnan Restaurant

Rte 10, Lyme, N.H.

D'ARTAGNAN'S is ten minutes north of Hanover, located on the lower level of a renovated eighteenth-century building overlooking Hewes Brook. It's what you might call a destination restaurant, since a trip to its casually elegant, flower-scented dining rooms is reason enough to launch a journey. Owner-chef Peter Gaylor and his wife, pastry chef Rebecca Cunningham, have crafted a small gem here, using the freshest of ingredients to fashion an ever-changing prix-fixe menu that never bows to the tyranny of food trends. Why blacken a poor fish, when it can be so deftly poached in a leek-studded sauce? A salmon mousseline torte makes us want to sign up for lessons. This is country dining at its best. **(603) 795-2137. Lunch Sun 12–1:15. Dinner Wed–Sun 6–9:15. Closed Mon–Tue. Reservations required. Expensive. AE.**

....

Home Hill

River Rd, Plainfield, N.H.

A CHATEAU on the river Loire it's not, but Home Hill is as close as you're apt to get to one in northern New England. This mansion set in a park was built in 1818, and several years ago Roger Nicolas, a Breton chef, made it his home. Veal is his particular specialty, but we can't think of a dish that disappoints. The only dilemma is deciding whether the chocolate mousse is better in its Belgian chocolate version or the Swiss. **(603) 675-6165. Dinner Tue–Sat 6–9. Closed Sun–Mon. Reservations required. Expensive. MC, V.**

....

Ivy Grill

Main St, Hanover, N.H.

D ARTMOUTH COLLEGE owns the Hanover Inn, and although the setting is rather grand, the food and service have traditionally been strictly sophomore. But in 1986 the inn's old coffee shop was replaced by the Ivy Grill, complete (at dinner) with its own chef and sous-chef. In Boston you'd pay twice as much for smoked trout this good, or for the equally excellent charred top sirloin with soy, ginger, and scallions.

Guests who stay an extra night to try the Rockport mussels and barbecued pork loin might just decide this food is worth matriculating for. **(603) 643-4300. Lunch daily 11:30–2. Light menu 2–5:30. Dinner 5:30–10. Moderate. AE, DC, MC, V.**

....

Prince and the Pauper

24 Elm St, Woodstock, Vt.

W E LIKE almost everything French on the menu of this small, recherché restaurant in Vermont's most pretentious small town. What thrills us less is the too-ambitious addition of other cuisines. The shrimp tempura is too nearly shrimp "limpura," and heavily cinnamoned acorn squash makes a startling Yankee intrusion into an already diverse mix of flavors. But don't take these complaints *too* seriously. This is quality food served by knowledgeable people in outstandingly pleasant surroundings. **(802) 457-1818. Dinner Sun–Thur 6–9, Fri–Sat until 9:30. Closed Mon. Reservations recommended. Expensive. MC, V.**

....

Rosalita's Southwestern Bar and Grill

Rte 4, Quechee, Vt.

T HERE is a covered bridge in Quechee, which you would expect, and a pretty good Mexican restaurant, which you might not. Rosalita's Southwestern Bar and Grill is better than either its misnomer or northeastern location suggests. The guacamole, nicely spiced and textured, is two cuts above the usual green paste. The *chalupa* entrée (tortilla, refried beans, beef, and rice) leans a trifle heavily on garlic, but at $4.95 it's a great buy. Even the hokey Margarita Pie is a treat. **(802) 295-1600. Lunch daily 11:30–3. Dinner 5–10. Light menu 3–5, 10–11. Moderate. AE, MC, V.**

....

Roberts' Country Cookin'

Rte 5, East Thetford, Vt.

HUMBLE, honest food you won't get at this rural diner, because the people who operate Roberts' Country Cookin' are not humble. They can even be rude. They run a local institution, and they know it. About fifty percent of the food is excellent. Skip the french fries — skip the fried food altogether. Go for breakfast, and order their exceptional bacon alongside French toast with maple syrup *du pays*. Go anytime, and tuck into the baked beans and stunning array of pies. You'll be too busy eating to be bothered by your server's attitude. **(802) 785-2990. Mon–Thur 6 a.m.–8 p.m.; Fri–Sat until 9; Sun 8 a.m.–3 p.m. Inexpensive. N.**

....

Shanghai Garden

129 Clinton St, Springfield, Vt.

SHANGHAI GARDEN, like a fortune cookie message, is simple, direct, and optimistic. Two Cantonese brothers and their sister run this homey Chinese diner with wooden booths and tie-back curtains on the industrial fringes of small-town Vermont. May their number increase. The Kung Pao Beef is paralyzingly hot, and even the *mooshi* pork is lively. Roam through the large menu, avoid the Americanized items, and be rewarded with copious dishes produced nearly as quickly as fast food. Dimmed lights and Asian music mellow the dinner hour. **(802) 885-5555. Beer and wine. Tue–Sun 11:30–10. Closed Mon. Reservations recommended. Inexpensive to moderate. N.**

Stone Soup

On the Green, Stratford, Vt.

THE STONE SOUP might seem to be only a chip off the old Cambridge block, but in fact it fits very nicely in this small Vermont village. Besides the regular yunnans — intelligently steamed casseroles — there is, as one might expect, an exceptional vegetarian lasagna. Pasta of such lightness is rare anywhere, and in this elegant folk-art setting, it's practically transporting. **(802) 765-4301. Dinner Wed–Sun 6–9. Closed Mon–Tue. Moderate. N, checks.**

The Third Rail

52 Main St (Rte 5), Fairlee, Vt.

NOT ALL good restaurants look upscale. Take The Third Rail, located on the main street of a rather homely Vermont village. The bare wooden tables and local accents dominating the room bespeak solid but unimaginative steak and seafood. But you'll be pleasantly surprised to find truly elegant baked sole, expertly cooked rice, and an appetizer of smoked salmon, sable, and trout arranged as deftly as if you were in Kyoto instead of along the Connecticut River. Good baking, too. **(802) 333-9797. Lunch Tue–Sat 11:30–2:30. Dinner Tue–Sat 5–10. Sun brunch 10–2. Closed Mon. Expensive. AE, DC, MC, V.**

....

THE BEST SANDWICHES in the region are found at **Peter Christian's** (39 South Main St, Hanover, N.H.), along with a very fine beef stew . . . The best soup, on the other hand, may be at the organically inclined **Soup Spoon** (57 North Park St, Lebanon, N.H.), which also has a nifty second-floor view of the city square . . . Try the **Courtyard Cafe** in the Hopkins Center at Dartmouth College (on the Green, Hanover, N.H.) for frozen yogurt and ice cream . . . If you're traveling with kids. **The Waterworks** (Power House Shopping Mall, West Lebanon, N.H.) has good chicken wings and desserts . . . Bright star on the horizon: the **Parker House Inn & French Restaurant** (Main St, Quechee, Vt.), recently reopened under the management of Roger Nicolas, owner of the incomparable Home Hill.

Burlington & Green Mountains

Austrian Tea Room

Trapp Family Lodge, Luce Hill Rd, Stowe

TAKE YOUR GUESTS from Ohio to lunch at the Austrian Tea Room on the grounds of the Trapp Family Lodge. Ideal for such visits, it offers a creditable Black Forest Cake and a breathtaking hilltop view alive with *The Sound of Music*. In summer, there are flowers and a deck; in fall, foliage spreads like a carpet; in winter, it's a living Christmas card. Waitresses in traditional costume serve up a mellow cheddar-cheese soup, dense, creamy potato salad, and just-fine knockwurst. Finish the meal off with big wedges of Linzer torte and Sacher torte, and you can't miss. Extra bonus: the best cross-country ski trails in Vermont. **(802) 253-8511. Daily 10:30–5:30, July–Oct until 8. Call for hours in Apr, Nov, and Dec. Inexpensive to moderate. Cr.**

The Daily Planet

15 Center St, Burlington

THE DAILY PLANET, widely considered Burlington's hippest bar and restaurant, is as welcoming as your own kitchen. The ratio of food to decor is a refreshing ten to three, with an emphasis on nouvelle combinations, oriental preparations (on Saturday nights there's a sushi bar), and pasta. Eclectic, in this case, doesn't mean eccentric; each dish is well seasoned and prettily presented. We especially like the cold Chinese noodles in spicy sesame sauce, the chicken with hot Thai flavors, and the Philly cheese steak sandwich. And the crowds tell you everyone else does, too. **(802) 862-9647. Lunch Mon–Sat 11:30–3. Dinner Sun–Thur 5–10:30, Fri–Sat until 11. Reservations recommended for six or more. Moderate. Cr.**

Hapleton's West Branch Cafe

Main St, Stowe

EATING OUT in downtown Stowe can get pretty esoteric, but fortunately Hapleton's West Branch Cafe is around for the locals and others who prefer serious eating to ultra-refined dining. Opened several years ago by two ski-lodge refugees, this diminutive basement hideout prides itself on its fine wines served by the glass, its ever-changing menu, and the equal care given to preparation of both the specials and the staples. From calamari with freshly made red-bell-pepper pasta to an offbeat combination of shrimp and veal (today's surf and turf?), the food delights. And in Stowe, where prices can be an embarrassment to propriety, this basement is a bargain. **(802) 253–4653. Sun–Fri 11:30 a.m.– 2 a.m., Sat until 1 a.m. No reservations. Moderate. Cr.**

Ice House
171 Battery St, Burlington

T HE ICE HOUSE is a place for all seasons. In the summer months it orients towards the lake. When it's cold outside, the basement level, with its stone walls and rough-hewn beams, seems a benevolent cave. The offerings, while pleasing to the eye and the palate, have been pared down to the basics: fish and meat, with several nightly specials. Thickly sliced pâté arranged around crusty French bread with a dollop of coarse mustard on the side is a winning starter, and we certainly can't carp about the seafood stew. The best advice: plan ahead for the three-layer Chocolate Chocolate Torte. **(802) 864–1800. Lunch daily 11:30–2:30. Dinner daily 5–10. Sun brunch 10:30–2:30. Reservations recommended. Expensive. Cr.**

Mary's
11 Main St, Bristol

G OING TO Mary's involves two emotions: first there's the nagging fear it has changed, and then comes warm satisfaction upon discovery that it hasn't. Driving past the Lord's Prayer Rock onto Main Street, you'll see the hand-carved sign over the storefront and dreamily recall a brunch of pumpkin soup with roasted garlic or apple-pear blintzes with creamy ricotta on the side. Mary's offers an understated ambience that balances sophisticated food with ad hoc furniture. **(802) 453-2432. Lunch Tue–Sat 11:30–3:30. Dinner Tue–Sat 5–9:30, Sun from 4. Sun brunch 10:30–3. Closed Mon and Columbus Day–Memorial Day. Moderate to expensive. Cr.**

....

Mary B.'s Tables

**12 Railroad Ave,
Essex Junction**

SURELY IT'S the American Way: pie from real pumpkins and a whistle-blowing iron horse rolling by the plate-glass windows. Such is the pleasure at Mary B.'s Tables, wainscotted and hung with quilts and close by the Amtrak station. The hummus plate includes thick homemade wheat bread and serves two. Fresh linguine with mussels and fresh vegetables is a delight — ditto the crispy vegetable tempura. Breads and desserts are also sold takeout. If we can't save Amtrak, let's at least save Mary B.'s. **(802) 879-4627. Mon–Fri 7–9, Sat 8–2 and 5–9. Closed Sun. Moderate. DC, MC, V.**

....

Pauline's

**1834 Shelburne Rd,
South Burlington**

THE STRIP DEVELOPMENT on Route 7 doesn't prepare you for Pauline's, a tiny restaurant on Burlington's southern fringes, that serves some of the best cuisine in the region. In the simply decorated upstairs dining room, the food stars. Subtly seasoned and beautifully presented appetizers, such as salmon terrine with caviar and fiddlehead-and-morel sauté, are worth more than supporting roles. Favorite entrées are grilled swordfish with tarragon hollandaise and thin slices of lamb with Vermont *chèvre*. It's rare to be able to savor every mouthful of a meal. **(802) 862-1081. Lunch Mon–Sat 11:30–2. Dinner Sun–Thur 5:30–9:30, Fri–Sat until 10. Sun brunch 10:30–3. Café menu available. Reservations accepted. Moderate to very expensive. Cr.**

Perry's Fish House

1080 Shelburne Rd, South Burlington

P ERRY'S FISH HOUSE looks as though it washed up from Maine on the simulated shore of Burlington's lakefront. But buoys, driftwood, and anchors do not a seafood restaurant make. The proof is on the plate, and *can* these people cook fish. Perry's selection, which changes daily, is unmatched hereabouts. The monkfish, salmon, and scrod are moist and flavorful; the family-style salad of non-iceberg greens is an uncommon accompaniment. Only the foil-wrapped baked potato is off-key. Nuns at a New York State convent make the cheesecake. Bless them. **(802) 862-1300. Dinner Mon–Thur 5–10; Fri–Sat until 11; Sun 4–10. Reservations recommended. Moderate to expensive. Cr.**

The Phoenix

Sugarbush Village, Warren

THE PHOENIX at Hotel Sugarbush features a friendly staff, serviceable steak, and an apple-glazed roast duckling that approaches excellence. But the entrées at this little two-tiered restaurant are merely preludes to dessert, two calorie-laden carts drawn through a tangle of tables. The triple-chocolate pie featured Swiss white chocolate mousse and shaved Belgian white chocolate atop a rich black cookie crust. The hazelnut torte is sheer intemperance. **(802) 583-2777. Open daily 6–10. Reservations recommended. Expensive. Cr.**

Rosemarie's

Rtes 17 and 116, Bristol

FOR TERRIFIC Italian food in a motel, there's Rosemarie's. The uniformed waitresses encourage you to experiment. Fried calamari is an enormous, crisp pile. The escarole and bean soup elevates those humble vegetables. You've probably not had conch (*scungilli* in marinara sauce) in a motel before, but such are the surprising pleasures here. **(802) 453-2326. Sun–Thur 5–9, Fri–Sat until 10. Closed Tue. Nov–Apr, closed Mon–Tue. Moderate to expensive. MC, V.**

Rusty Scuffer

148 Church St, Burlington

THE SOUND OF munching through food trends is heard in Church Street Marketplace, but not at the Rusty Scuffer. In this fifteen-year-old family-run spot, the bare wood tables are crowded with people eating the way they used to and for the same tiny tab. It's strictly barnboard-and-seventies time warp, but pleasantly achieved when steak or lobster dinners go for under ten dollars. If the baked potato is a bit underdone, the dense fish chowder is fine, the steak rare, and the boiled lobster a respectable size. **(802) 864-9451. Mon–Thur 11–10, Fri–Sat until 11. Moderate. CB, DC, MC, V.**

Sweetwater's

120 Church St, Burlington

S OME FOODS have more cachet than others, but Sweetwater's tries to keep tabs on them all. Potato skins and nachos long ago attained staple status here, and mesquite-broiled chicken, oriental stir-fry, and blackened redfish are vying for similar recognition. Sometimes the management will even glue several trends together, as in chicken fingers, tempura-style, in a pita pocket. None of this food is bad, especially when sampled on a summer evening while people-watching from their fine sidewalk café. But its wild diversity leaves the feeling that Sweetwater's is married more to fashion than to character. **(802) 864-9800. Lunch Mon–Sat 11:30–5. Dinner Sun–Thur 5–10, Fri–Sat until 11. Late-night menu Mon–Sat until 12:30. Sun brunch 10:30–3. Reservations recommended. Moderate. Cr.**

Ten Acres Lodge

Barrows Rd, Stowe

I N VERMONT, tradition means more than folksy prints and common crackers. Ten Acres Lodge, a charming old farmhouse first opened as a winter ski lodge in the 1940s, maintains the traditions that have built Stowe's gustatory reputation: an intimate, un-stuffy atmosphere, creative chefs, and quiet, professional service. The rather petite portion of soft-shell crab in savory garlic-lemon sauce is nonetheless tantalizing, and the chef's combination of yellowfin tuna, halibut, sea scallops, and asparagus is encumbered by nothing more than a delicate beurre blanc. You'll need the energizing effect of a double shot of espresso, or you may never get up from the table. **(802) 253-7638. Dinner daily 6–9:30. Reservations recommended. Very expensive. Cr.**

Tubbs

24 Elm St, Montpelier

T UBBS, a tastefully appointed lab-oratory for second-year student chefs at the New England Culinary Institute, tries for postgraduate glamour when a studious competence would suffice. Because chefs change weekly, the food is uneven, and the service can seem amateur. On various occasions, we've been served a sublime monk-fish, a quite nice confit of duck, and an absolutely appalling veal shank. Still, this is the place to see genius in the making, and you may be lucky enough to land the valedictorian. **(802) 229-9202. Lunch Mon–Fri 11:30–2. Dinner Mon–Sat 6–9:30. Reservations recommended. Expensive. Cr.**

....

Tucker Hill Lodge

Rte 17, Waitsfield

IN THE Green Mountains, good reputations are hard to come by and harder still to keep, and yet after ten years Tucker Hill Lodge remains unsullied. Intimates can share quiet corner cubbies while noisier revelers hoist their glasses in the front alcove, and the fare, which changes daily, is elegance itself. New Zealand pompano steamed in a cunning parchment fan gives good indication of the kitchen's talents, as does the thick wedge of Norwegian salmon enveloped in a buttery golden crust. The flourless chocolate cake, however, is more daring than delicious. **(802) 496-3983. Daily 6–9:30. Reservations recommended. Very expensive. Cr.**

....

The Village Pump House Restaurant

Falls Rd, Shelburne

DINING AT The Village Pump House Restaurant, located in a small turn-of-the-century house on the town green, is like dining with friends — but only if they've hired a fine chef. Everything in the two tiny rooms plus sun porch is on a domestic scale, hosted by a chef who went public with his home cooking. With soft, recorded chamber music, convivial chatter from the bar (imported beers are a specialty), and a menu that concentrates on classic preparations of well-sauced seafood, filet mignon, and veal, you can sit back in your cane chair and smile with satisfaction. But don't forget the Granny Smith Apple Cake. **(802) 985-3728. Lunch Tue–Sat 11:30–2. Dinner Tue–Thur 5:30–9:30, Fri–Sat until 10. Closed Sun–Mon. Reservations recommended. Expensive. Cr.**

....

Villa Tragara

Rte 100, Waterbury Center

NOTHING WARMS the spirit better than northern Italian cooking, and northern New Englanders need it even more than the Italians do. Warm feelings come easily at Villa Tragara, especially when one is seated at a candlelit window table in this restored farmhouse restaurant. Savoring a plate of mussels in a tomato-basil broth so good you scoop up every drop, we wondered if the rest of the meal could measure up. Not to worry. The same subtlety and care marked the fresh Pasta Mista — a trio of excellent veal ravioli, fettuccine Alfredo, and pearly *gnocchi* — and the fork-tender veal, stuffed with fontina and prosciutto in a dark mushroom sauce. Bravo! **(802) 244-5288. Dinner Tue–Sun 5:30–9:30. Closed Mon. Reservations recommended. Moderate to expensive. AE, MC, V.**

....

What's Your Beef

152 Paul St, Burlington

WHAT'S YOUR BEEF answers the question splendidly. Deservedly celebrated as Burlington's great red-meat house, this cozy rathskeller chockablock with tables offers generous prime rib and a filet mignon that is precisely charcoaled, rich, and juicy. Sure, you can opt for seafood — the scallops are adequate, the sole sufficient — but it's best to save this spot for times when you have a high-cholesterol hankering. **(802) 862-0326. Dinner Mon–Thur 4–10; Fri–Sat 4:30–10:30; Sun 4:30–9:30. No reservations. Moderate. DC, MC, V.**

Woody's

5 Bakery Ln, Middlebury

FANTASY ARCHITECTURE and pampered food are the order of the day at Woody's, a tidy, peach-tinged art deco oceanliner of a restaurant overlooking Otter Creek. The cooking here is always elegant, often innovative. We succumbed to poached Norwegian salmon with dill hollandaise, and pan-darkened Cajun shrimp, the latter from an interesting light-entrée menu. Chocolate is an art here, but this time we tried the homemade ice cream and weren't sorry. Service is up to Cunard standards. **(802) 388-4182. Lunch Mon–Sat 11:30–3. Dinner Mon–Sat 5–10. Sun brunch 10:30–3. Light menu daily 3–12. Reservations recommended. Moderate to expensive. AE, DC, MC, V.**

Waking up is a lot nicer knowing **Sneakers Bar & Grill** (36 Main St, Winooski) is making the eggs Benedict . . . At **Jana's Cupboard** (Rtes 15 and 108, Jeffersonville) breakfast is served until 1 p.m. on weekends; order the blueberry flapjacks . . . Fans of Pauline's are bullish on **Déjà Vu** (185 Pearl St, Burlington), under the same ownership and featuring a promising new chef; French-inspired food in a wonderful wood and brass sanctum . . . Good fresh pasta at the **Vt. Pasta Co.** (156 Church St, Burlington) . . . The **Five Spice Café** (175 Church St, Burlington) has a very fine (and often spicy) stir-fry.

Southern
Vermont

Brasserie

324 County St, Bennington

SURELY SOMEONE should notify Guinness? The menu at the Brasserie (in Bennington's charming Potter's Yard) is one hundred percent Cajun-free — in fact, the café's offerings have scarcely wavered since Dione Lucas opened this culinary class act back in the sixties. The staple remains French peasant fare, like the Snack de Provence sandwich featuring a warm onion jam. Although the decor is white-wall stark, the mood is small-town convivial. **(802) 447-7922. Mon–Sat 11:30–8, Sun from 10:30. No reservations. Moderate. MC, V.**

Casa Bianca

76 Grove St, Rutland

DINNER AT Casa Bianca is rather like going home to Mother. Two small dining rooms have an atmosphere that's intimate, serene, and candlelit. Among an eclectic assortment of Italian specialties, homemade bean and spinach soup is hearty, veal parmigiana is fork tender, and home-baked rolls are above average. If salad lettuce must be iceberg, an excellent vinaigrette dressing on tender center leaves is acceptable. However, Sanka instead of brewed decaf isn't. **(802) 773-7401. Tue–Sat 6–9. Closed Sun–Mon. Reservations recommended. Expensive. MC, V.**

....

Common Ground Community Restaurant

25 Elliot St, Brattleboro

THE Common Ground Community Restaurant is a Peter Pan of a place. Established in 1971, it was the first (and now the last) of the natural-food, mostly vegetarian, co-operative eateries in the area. It hasn't changed a bit: same airy and ramshackle atmosphere, same honey and tamari on the tables, even many of the same customers. The food tends to be substantial rather than subtle, but it's admirably cheap: prices range from the ninety-cent Humble Bowl of Rice to nine-dollar entrées, with a heavy emphasis on ethnic food. Menus change seasonally, but a recommended perennial is the vegetable pastry du jour. As we left, the Beatles were suggesting we "let it be." We hope this place never grows up. **(802) 257-0855. Beer and wine. Lunch Wed–Mon 11:30–2:30. Dinner Wed–Mon 5:30–8. Sun brunch 10:30–1:30. Closed Tue. Inexpensive. N.**

....

Curtis' Barbeque

Rte 5, Putney

URTIS' BARBEQUE may not be, as several hand-painted signs immodestly proclaim, "the ninth wonder of the world," but it certainly is a marvel, a bit of the bayou flourishing off I-91. From this royal-blue school bus (permanently parked in a grove beside a gas station) issue ribs and chicken of the first rank, tantalizingly browned over a slow wood fire and subdued to fall-off-the-bone tenderness. As for sauce, Curtis eschews the namby-pamby gummy-sweet school in favor of vinegary and vitriolic — the kind that makes your eyes tear, your nose run. He could teach the Thais a thing or two. **(802) 387-5474. Thur–Sun 10 a.m.–dark. Closed in winter. Inexpensive. N.**

Four Columns Inn

West St, Newfane

ISITING A RENOWNED four-star restaurant for lunch can be as discomfiting as calling on a socialite midmorning only to find her *en peignoir*. Like most formidable dowagers, the Four Columns Inn has two faces. One appears in a menu geared to travelers easily contented with a ham-and-cheese sandwich. The other is hinted at in the daily special: a perfectly sautéed soft-shell crab in a clever setting of eminently edible seaweed (it's called *poussepied* and resembles fresh, young *haricots verts*). That and dessert, superb tortes and tarts, have induced us to do the right thing and return for dinner, when the grande dame gets all dolled up. **(802) 365-7713. Jackets. Dinner Wed–Mon 6–9. Closed Tue. Lunch July–Oct; call for hours. Reservations recommended. Very expensive. MC, V.**

....

The Inn at Long Last

Main St, Chester

NEW OWNERSHIP has nicely refitted the fine old Chester Inn, and rechristened it The Inn at Long Last. The crackling fire in the spacious foyer, the cozy library lounge, and the elegant touches in the dining room are what separate this place from the ordinary. The fixed-price menu can do the classics well (salmon was nicely grilled in a garlic-herb butter), but what's most impressive is the inventive use of herbs: in a mushroom bisque laced with basil, and veal and prosciutto sauced with fennel. Unfortunately, the dessert list is trite, the coffee generic, and the all-American wine list needlessly chauvinistic. **(802) 875-2444. Dinner Tue–Thur 6–8, Fri–Sat until 9; Sun 11:30–2. Moderate to expensive. AE, MC, V.**

....

Londonderry Inn

Rte 100, South Londonderry

THE DECOR augurs haute-HoJo, tops. But dinners at the Londonderry Inn are steadfastly thrilling, substantial yet worldly. With little fanfare and no observable fuss, this kitchen has turned out exemplary duckling, savory sage-stuffed veal, and a tender pork saté that have inspired many return visits. Country inns tend to engender certain expectations regarding comfort and graciousness; despite the copper lanterns and plaid curtain cliché, this one delivers on the dream. **(802) 824-5226. Dinner Wed–Mon 6:30–9:30. Closed Tue. Expensive. N, personal checks.**

....

Longwood Inn

Rte 9, Marlboro

DINING AT THE Longwood Inn promises a heavenly match of eclectic, creative cuisine in a warm, traditional setting. We thought we knew mussels inside out, but previous renditions are rawhide dog-toys compared to these: sliced crosswise, simmered to the consistency of foie gras, and tossed with angel-hair pasta blackened with squid ink and heaped with mashed garlic. Bliss in every bite — and a blackboard's worth of promises still to go. **(802) 257-1545. Breakfast 8–10. Dinner 5:30–9. Sun brunch 11–3. Reservations recommended. Expensive. MC, V.**

....

Village Auberge

Rte 30, Dorset

A BEAUTIFUL little inn, Village Auberge removes the stigma from the term *continental* and restores the charm. Although each dish is classically executed, the effect is that favored by innovators: clarion flavors, true and intense. The lobster mousse is pâté of pincer, fluffy but not frothy; the miniature cheese fritters are tiny clouds of raclette. The only place the flavor-distillation process backfires is in the salty pork *en croûte* — but when was the last time you could complain of said substance being too savory? The setting, a bowfront parlor with botanical motifs, is serene, the hospitality all-pervasive. **(802) 867-5715. Dinner Tue–Sun 6–9. Closed Mon. Reservations recommended. Very expensive. AE, MC, V.**

. . . .

T HE **Three Clock Inn** (Middletown Rd, South Londonderry) may be the only place in the state to have authentic *pomme frites* . . . At the **Old Newfane Inn** (on the Green, Newfane), shun the carriage-trade staples (duckling and the like) for seasonal treats such as cream-of-fiddlehead soup . . . We can never pass up the pierogi at **Saxton's River Inn** (Main St, Saxton's River), nor keep from peeking at the old iron stove where a dozen outstanding desserts are displayed.